HOCKEY in the Blood

Gavin Featherstone

Faaronheigt Publishing

Hockey in the Blood

Published by Faaronheigt Publishing

ISBN 978-0-9935266-1-9

© 2018 Gavin Featherstone

A catalogue record for this book is available from the British Library.

Printed and distributed in the UK by Witley Press Ltd.,
24-26 Greevegate, Hunstanton PE36 6AD.
www.witleypress.co.uk

Hockey in the Blood is available from Amazon Books at amazon.co.uk

Contents

Once upon a time,
when the Thames touched the Tyne..........

This book is dedicated to the life of Peter Charles.

Introduction

I have news for all those executives of the FIH and the IOC, our sport of hockey is not there to be messed with. They must ask themselves as the latest pronouncement is made like the white smoke above the Vatican if they are taking the hockey world with them. 'Hockey in the Blood' is the antidote to all their international meddling lording it over the grass roots of our game.

The book is a celebration of those events and personalities that have made, and do make the game tick at all levels. There is presented to the reader stories of human struggle, despair and triumph that many may very well identify with. I have tried to highlight in these pages the love and affection that hockey people share for their sport across the globe.

The chapters focus on the lives of great characters in hockey that seldom are written about or even recognised. The book concentrates on the conflict they have faced in dealing with another option, another obsession or distraction which has competed with hockey for supremacy. Fame, greed, crime, sibling rivalry, religion, and walks on the wild side spring to mind

The chapters are completely unrelated, the common thread being my privileged association with all of the hockey men and women involved with the narrative. The reader must forgive me to have inserted nicknames and assumed identities at times, but all the events reflect very true issues and events that have hit the hockey world over the last five decades. Some are heart warming, many eccentric and humorous. Then there are the sad and dark ones flirting with controversy.

I have attempted to embrace the lot. Our great game would not expect anything less from me!

No excuses, Gavin Featherstone

Sincere Thanks

The author would like to express his hockey-felt gratitude to the following inmates for their willing and invaluable help and support for the writing of this book. Ribenas on me!

Cheers:

Paul Sorensen: 'the best right half never to have played for England'.

Kerry Moore: 'the dribbling Queen of Olton and W.W."

Neil Mallett: 'Brummie through and through!"

Kelvyn Skee: Komputer King of KS Digital.

and also, for the contribution of:

Hackney Libraries Archives

Just Hockey, Australia

The Abina Hotel, Amstelveen

Battersea Public Library Archives

Charles Lawrence Sports Surfaces

The 1890 Bar/Restaurant, Amsterdam

Photographs gratefully supplied by:

Millfield School, Somerset

Harendra Singh, India's National Coach

Helge Schutz in Windhoek

Jacky Bates, PA to the Bishop of Sherwood

Tobias von de Haar Bahniuk

The Homerton House Coaching Collection

Peter Luck of Hockey Digest

Folkestone Borough Council

Foreword

Having known the author for many years, as a player, coach and often life mentor, I am delighted Gavin has eventually taken the time to sit down and capture some of the quite amazing stories he has been involved in. These cross the many eras and locations that encompass the passion, lifelong involvement and often bizarre opportunities the world of Hockey has brought to the young, veterans, male and female alike.

Gavin is a man of great kindness, who has achieved much in our sport as a recognised International player and coach, however it is his ability to remember the 'little people' in hockey, who do so much for so little reward or recognition that always impressed me and I'm glad to see he has included a few stories about the people at the grass roots of our sport, who give so much of their lives to help others achieve great things on the world stage, as well as surprising encounters with some of the world's best in unusual circumstances.

Considering everything the author has achieved and continues to achieve and influence within our sport, he is not afraid to face the broad realities of the sport, whether he is covering situations that are as diverse as the glory assumed by the top international stars or to issues which many people prefer not to acknowledge out in the open.

Gavin, many would agree, is in a fortunate position to provide a commentary in a most entertaining manner as a result of his broad areas of expertise within the game at all levels worldwide.

I hope you enjoy reading the book, as much as I have enjoyed reading the varied and unrelated chapters as they were being written.

Harry Dunlop *High Performance (Head) Hockey Coach.*
Glasgow School of Sport, National Centre of Excellence

Chapter 1

Gold

Lav cut inside from just outside the 25-yard line, hung out a yo-yo for the last English defender to bite, then duly rounded the leaden-footed Featherstone. Now with only the keeper to beat, he angled his run diagonally into the circle and flipped it past his right pad into the corner.

Yugoslavia, yes Yugo who? They had just equalised after being three goals down to a young, experimental England team in a full international at the Folkestone Festival. The white surrounding chalk hills had provided the backdrop to the shock of the day as many of the English players never even knew Yugoslavia played the game.

Lav Pavlovic was part of a national team in the late 70s that had competed strongly within the 'B' Division of European nations seldom gaining the chance to play against the 'big boys'. Yet he knew he was good, very good, as he had in the previous 18 months scored against West and East Germany and Poland. Yugoslavia, then made up of seven future nations, was well known for its football and basketball prowess, but the sport of hockey was mainly confined to what now would be known as Croatia and Slovenia.

The amalgamation of seven states was held together by Marshall Tito in these years but as he was very advanced in years, what then of the provinces of Macedonia, Bosnia, Serbia and the remainder when he did pass on?

Lav was very wary of the future, aware of the diverse nature of the Balkan States in terms of religion and culture. Still, he had enjoyed five good years in the national and international limelight of contesting test matches against the West and the East. More to the point, he was young and single and had a passport that was valid in Western Europe and to the states behind Churchill's "Iron Curtain", the Eastern bloc.

He was truly joyful on hearing the news that he could display his skills at the world-famous Folkestone Festival at the end of the winter season. Independently run by Nevil and Barbara Miroy, the Festival in association with "The Optimists' Club", represented not only over 50 years of Easter competition for British clubs, but also acted as the gateway to England for

European clubs and national teams, and in 1979 Yugoslavia joined the USA as international guests of the Festival of hockey.

It was the pinnacle of his standards. There was to be little frolicking here with informal and formal international games played as well as the highlight of the weekend. The Miroys would select an All-Star Squad to play against the most prestigious of the European club teams normally from Belgium, the Netherlands or the then West Germany. To the everyday player though, they would crowd into the twelve pitches simultaneously battling it out for a result to celebrate in the packed hotels on the Leas Seafront just a mile away later in the evenings.

The England team, very disgruntled after only drawing with Yugoslavia, donned their blazers and trudged to the drinks reception hosted by the Miroys, a small banquet to welcome the overseas guests. The usual round of speeches and exchanges of gifts gave way to much merriment fuelled by a generous supply of champagne, wine and copious mixes and mixtures of every drink imaginable.

England's players were let off the leash for the evening, but it was no surprise to see them 'on the wagon' the entire evening. True reports about only drawing the game, if supplemented by tales of over the top drinking meant only one thing – abstinence.

The opposite could only apply to a Yugoslav team in the top gear of celebration. Here they were away from a declining economic dip at home with a poor future for employment, so they were going to milk this one like there was no tomorrow. Lav was no stranger to the demon drink, but he happened to have the best command of the English language from his university days in Zagreb.

He was on a mission. He wanted out from Tito's Yugoslavia and the terrible prospect of a communist takeover in Croatia. Surely here was a chance to network and find a way of playing or coaching in the West. So many blazers represented wealth and influence in one room. To him it meant opportunity.

His intent was met when he confronted the very same English team "gentleman", the one that after the game had remarked, "Thanks for the game, mate, one of the best goals scored against us in years." As on the field, he struck up a meaningful two-way conversation about the real chance of competing in a club team with hopefully a job offer alongside it. That was essential, as in 1979, it was nigh on impossible to be paid to play. Hockey stuck rigidly to its amateur code, a factor that Lav just could not comprehend. After all, basketball was also an Olympic sport, and there was an active Pro-Basketball league in Yugoslavia.

"There may be some irons in the fire I can look into, but whatever, I will see you at the Tournament Dinner later this week, okay?"

Lav only picked up the 'future meeting', what the hell was the Brit talking about "irons and fire" for?

He was to find out at the Tournament Dinner, a 'lavish' occasion with over 12 nations represented at over 80 tables set for a five-course spread. Again, the boys from Belgrade, Zagreb and Sarajevo piled into the culinary treat with ample liquid sustenance. They had never experienced such hospitality in the dull drab world of austerity that was Eastern Europe in 1979.

Lav spotted his English friend anew, joining with a group of fellow countrymen with bright scarlet ties with a frontage of a beer mug crossing through a heart. They were representing an invitation team and club called "The Lady Killers". This was explained to Lav, who never could understand the English humour that called such great teams such derogatory names like, "The Tramps", "The Llamas" and the "Hairy Goats".

Enough of the small talk, the English international had come up with the goods. It wasn't exactly what Lav had wanted, but all the same it was incredibly tempting. It was not to play and coach in England, but in far away sunny South Africa. The English player had already acted as a go-between for Lav and one of South Africa's greatest players, who had been playing at the Festival for one of the invitational club teams. He, of course, could do this as there was no international programme for the banned sports teams from apartheid South Africa.

Our good Samaritan from the southern hemisphere was to offer an 8-month winter employment deal with a Goldfields club from the Western Transvaal who wanted a sports officer to oversee the newly created role for the training of not just potential hockey, but also football players from Westonaria Deep. But could Lav play football?

The answer was emphatically yes, as he had represented his university as a footballer as well and even had a Preliminary Level 1 badge for football as a trainer! Lav then learned that there were no visa problems, his accommodation was part of the job and his salary was three times what he was earning as an assembly worker in darkest Zagreb. In his wildest dreams, he never thought that the irons or the fire could turn up something as good as this in such a short time.

He had to think hard that night. He was only a year away from the Moscow Olympics, but Yugoslavia were nowhere near that event, even if the rumour was true about a possible 'western' boycott. No, he was guaranteed a sports officer job the following January which meant he had eight months to clear his desk in Zagreb, and that was forever.

Lav left the dinner to his overexuberant mates thanking the benevolence of his new English friend that had given him all the prospective names and addresses to contact with a glowing reference from both himself and the mysterious South African.

He made his way back to the Northcliffe Hotel bar which was pretty isolated as the teams were all still at the reception. He ordered himself a bottle of white wine they called 'Blue Nun' from a petite barmaid. He insisted on her delivering it to his table, and was it him or the occasion, but he fathomed up enough courage to order two glasses.

Judy Warrington said she shouldn't, with what he observed as a twinkle in the eye. "All right then, just one, while no one is here," she enthused.

The one turned into three more than medium glasses. They had hit it off, lightning had struck twice all in one evening. She was so impressed with a gent that was intriguing and yet interested in her, only her. His Eastern European tones really fell on deaf ears as she had never been east of Ramsgate!

Lav had always been one for the ladies, but as of yet, hockey was his master and mistress. Most of the Zagreb girls had long since given up on him as they could spot a sportsman or any army man a mile off. A succession of one-night stands had left the ladies fumbling in the dark with no hope of anything more meaningful from the likes of Lav.

However, he liked what he saw in Judy and wanted to get to know her. He did get to achieve this in typical maverick fashion by deliberately missing his team flight from Heathrow to Belgrade on Tuesday. There were to be many repercussions, but by the following weekend when he had been reported missing to the Yugoslav Embassy, he handed himself into the special agents.

Still, he had achieved what he wanted, a week to secure a promising relationship with Judy.

She had that week smuggled him into her room that went with her uncle's family business. Luckily, he was willing for just four nights to relax the rules, but she would still lose her salary. Uncle Jim was sympathetic as she had been a really good worker since she left school at 18, two years earlier. With scanty qualifications, Judy was always telling him one day the hotel would be hers to run. All he would say was,

"In yer dreams, love!!"

She waved goodbye to Lav in a taxi that arrived at the hotel with two very drab, glum looking gents. He promised he would write, but she just prayed that he would, and would not be in any trouble. Uncle Jim had teased her that he was a spy from the East and that Judy had become one of his "Bond girls".

Folkestone, in hockey and work terms had lived up to its reputation of bringing sports people together under one roof. Little did the Miroys know that they were indirectly responsible for one of the greatest adventures any hockey exponent had undertaken across three dynamic cultures.

South-west of Johannesburg lies the Golden Arc which represents more than 15% of South Africa's total wealth. A huge broad deposit of alluvial remnants yielded surface rocks of gleaming mineral, but then dipped low across the Veld to expose the deepest gold mines in the world.

The Gold Rush of the last 19th Century had attracted individual prospectors, then associated groups to national concerns to the area known as the Witwatersrand – White Waters Ridge – with its new mecca, then a cowboy town termed Johannes-burg. Fortunes were sought, found and wasted in a town with that wild west feel about it. If the 'Arc' from Johannesburg dipping down to Welkom in the Orange Free State could be encapsulated into one word, that single word would be risk.

Lav was the late 19th Century's version of the multitudes that had trod this path before. He though, was not just in search of wealth from an unlikely source, sport, but he was escaping, also from the harsh realities of his mother country about to be split apart into fierce fighting.

As for sport, 1980 was a pivotal Olympic year with its focal point on Moscow, but he was to be positioned here far, far away in an ostracised banned country. South Africa was an international pariah, banned from sporting competition since 1970, but still a sports mad nation at every level. He knew all this and the likelihood of him being placed on the Anti-Apartheid blacklist. This in turn did not concern him as he had already resigned himself to sporting, playing retirement.

What he wanted most was reward and money for his efforts, enough from a one-off contract to set himself and Judy up for a future in the West.

* * * * *

The seat-belts sign lit up as he was inundated with thoughts lingering on Judy, whilst below, the waste dumps of glittering pale orange gold littered the dry landscape. With the penetrating early morning sun cascading through the 707's narrow slits of windows, he clenched his fists tight, ready to take on the biggest challenge of his life.

Mr Viljoen, the Personnel Director of his Associated Mine Group out in Westonaria was there to meet and greet the Yugoslav star at the then Jan Smuts Airport. All airports in the Republic were named after prominent politicians of the past, a kind of reminder to all arrivals of who was or were the bosses of the country. Viljoen displayed a cordial nature as his chauffeur driven Mercedes sped off around The Johannesburg Ring taking in views of the Central Business District from the south.

Lav had never seen anything like it. Movies had got through to him in Zagreb of New York City, but here is South Africa, surely this was the New York of the Southern Hemisphere. Dozens of skyscraper buildings towered into the thin air of 5,000 feet above sea level. All he could dream about was the wealth derived to the citizens, the white citizens of such a bonanza, all based on gold.

Not for one moment did he consider the plight of the native African, the black man.

It took the best part of an hour to reach the site of the mine on the road between Westonaria and Carletonville, a route which bypassed the sprawling South-West Townships, Soweto, the hub of the industrialised Witwatersrand's labour force.

Lav was shown to his quarters in a whites only residential single-storey block which he was to share with three other imported personnel for his stay of eight months. All white workers were either supervisors, technicians or accountants, but always definitely middle management. This contrasted sharply with the hordes of indented temporarily employed miners from all over sub-Saharan Africa as well as from the homelands of Xhosa, Sutu and Zulu tribal groups within South Africa.

Most of the workers, hundreds of whites and thousands of blacks, were there to ply their trade in shift work patterns which made the residential blocks places of repose and sleep and leisure. Yet the time schedules worked like clockwork allowing for late afternoon and early evening leisure activities. These active leisure hours were now available. It had been a long hard road to achieve them from a 24-hour work regime.

The black worker in the Gold Belt had not only faced up until the previous year a situation of non-existent trade unions, but an incredibly high fatality risk from poor safety records in this, one of the deepest mines in South Africa. The entire Gold Belt was recording record metric tons of the mineral between 1970 and 1980, yet until now unable to boast leisure facilities for its miners. This had all changed the previous year with the legalisation of black trade unions and collective bargaining, but with an interesting condition, no strikes!!

You may ask, with all the indentured labour from as far afield as Zambia, Zimbabwe, Mozambique and Australia, how did they communicate? A hybrid language built on Zulu, English and Afrikaans had penetrated down through the decades, and young Lav, or Leo as he was to be named around the football and hockey pitch leisure areas, would have to pick this up quickly.

Within a week, Leo was to face the rudimentary medical that every worker underwent, a thorough examination of body and teeth from specialists Dr Van Zyl and a rather eccentric dentist called Avi Silverman. Leo just wondered why he had to 'open wide' to display his rather disjointed set of molars.

All was pronounced fit and Leo soon got down to planning and organising the internal leagues for football and hockey to be played at the mine's 'Upper' and 'Lower' pitches during his tenure. Amazingly, both were great surfaces with regular groundsmen and to his delight, a collection of floodlit towers. Power was never a problem in this occupation.

His priority was to set up strict timetables, and a refereeing officiating system for every game. The two football fields on the 'Lower' meant that at any one time he had to have six officials, and six officials that were not "bent", as many of the teams were strictly tribal or national!! Hockey on the inevitable Upper was much easier as most of these middle-class employees were white

English-speaking specialists from the UK, Canada, Australia and for the most part, South Africa.

Coaching was to be developed. He had the idea that every team in the League, and there were over 20 football squads and eight hockey teams, had to self-appoint a specific off the field coach and manager. They, in turn, would have to come to Leo's coaching clinics held one a week.

The mine's employers rubberstamped his plans from his inaugural meeting. Just one more matter would pre-empt his eight-month contract.

"How would you like to be paid?" asked Mr Viljoen, "In Rand, Pounds, Dollars or Krugerrands?"

The final element was the South African gold coins eagerly sought after as an investment plan for the future. His roommate from the UK had explained to him that it was well worth looking into the Gold Standard, the international price for gold. He had checked the 'Rand Daily Mail's business section which was running continuing articles on the upward volatility of gold's value in 1980.

That, indeed, was an understatement. With the impact of the Iranian Ayatollah's revolution, the Russians invading Afghanistan and high inflation around the world, the mineral had reached a 20th Century high of $US 850 an ounce, in real terms the average price was estimated at $1,503 per ounce. So, with the Russians even building up their forces on his national country's border with Bulgaria, Leo made a prompt reply, as all the movers and shakers were moving to gold,

"Krugerrand, Mister Viljoen, please!"

Viljoen informed him that if he wished to take these coins out of the country, there would be a maximum demanded on export control, but he need not worry because the mine had a way of topping the coins up by other means. He fondly referred to this as the Krand bonus! Smiling at Leo, "If your plans for our leisure sector play out well, I will inform you nearer the time in August!"

Now down to work with the added bonus of a company paid phone call to Judy every Sunday evening, he took to his work like a duck to water. His superiors were really impressed not only by the improved activity and productivity levels of the workers, but also in the welfare and feelgood factor it engendered in the diverse groups of miners. Petty squabbles and thieving between tribal groups was declining and there was a genuine ambition in the men to play for their football and hockey teams. The mine's 'esprit de corps' had never been better, and it was a fact that this Amalgamated Mine Group acted as a precursor for many of the 'Golden Arcs' to follow.

Leo was in cloud cuckoo land. Food pretty good, although he never could get the hang of mielies, and Windhoek lager, but they were all to his liking. The leagues were a great success, and with everything paid for including one day clear a week to take visits to Pretoria and Johannesburg, he was finding the money he was earning was the money he was saving. He kept the marvellous gold coins in the company's PO Box, accumulating rapidly as the months ticked by.

He missed Judy so badly and in a strange sort of way the weekly phone calls brought them even closer together. Verbally they were planning for the future and having frequent discussions on a potential long term move to the Goldfields of South Africa, but he sensed all along that she was a home bird reluctant to leave her Kentish roots.

God, it was getting dry, and the Veldfields under Leo's jurisdiction were appearing paler and paler and bare from the sheer number of games played. It was early August and fast was approaching the termination of Leo's winter in the golden sun.

"Time for your medical," blurted Viljoen as indeed the obligatory departing assessments had to be made. Van Zyl hardly took more than twenty minutes to run through the heart, ear, lungs, eye and cardiovascular routines that were required on entry and exit to all workers.

"Now for Mister Silverman, Leo". The Croatian always smiled at the thought that a Jewish dentist called Silver-Man was working for a gold mine.

Silverman was exact and precise. With his young wife as the nurse, he barked out his observations as he explored Leo's inner mouth.

"Lower right 4, 6 and 8, Upper right, 4, 6 and 8, and the same on the left hand side, twelve cavities, you have been a naughty boy!"

"What!" cried Leo, "You are telling me I must have twelve fillings?"

Leo hated dentists at the best of times. After such a fantastic contract, was this to be the painful legacy from the Goldfields?

"I will do the lot for you, all on your day off, six in the morning and six in the afternoon, the K Rand Special!!" Leo was left wondering the sheer sadism, and in his case, the open masochism of virtually all his middle to back teeth being filled.

So it proved to be. An entire day of drilling was over by 4 pm that Friday afternoon. He never, never wanted to visit the dentist chair again.

"Get up and cast your eyes in the mirror," Silverman provided the specialised mirror which could show his inner teeth.

Leo just about fainted. He was bedazzled by four golden arcs! The sadist had filled his mouth full of gold!! It was truly amazing.

Now all you will have to do on return in two days' time will be to visit my brother, Manny, in Golders Green. He's the best dentist in North London.

"Immanuel will look after you, extract and weigh, even give you a price for our gold, and note the percentage in these bridges and fillings is exceedingly high, my boy," suggested the dental genius.

* * * * *

Judy had got to Heathrow just in time, roadworks everywhere, that Sunday morning to Terminal 3. The British Airways flight was on time and at the gate she was not late. She perused everyone that came through the revolving doors, but her attention was distracted by a guy that was holding up a placard reading "Mr Lav Pavlovic".

Leo burst through the doors, all over his future English rose, which took a full two minutes of reassuring embrace. He turned to spot his new to be friend,

"It's Manny, yeah, glad to meet you, when do you start your work? Avi sends his best!"

Judy was horrified, just who was this mysterious man from the London suburbs? She mused.

The three of them set off with the couple in the back seat preoccupied with Leo displaying a bag full of Krugerrands and proudly showing off his "golden arcs" to Judy.

She had no idea what her Croatian was on, nor could she understand why she was to spend the day at a dentist's surgery. By seven o'clock that evening, a weary Leo was to reveal all,

"Judy, would you be my K Rand bride?"

He then filled in the details of his remarkable stay on the Veld, and how he had amassed a small fortune. The answer was in her eyes,

"Yes, yes, but only if we can buy it."

"Buy what?" he quizzed.

"The Northcliffe, my uncle's hotel."

He had answered her dreams in every way, to run the Northcliffe, off the Leas in Folkestone. Now the two of them could be the hosts, every Easter, of hockey teams around the world. The two lovers would even have their wedding reception there.

The very next Monday morning, Lav Pavlovic opened the Financial Times weekly index.

It read: Gold reaches Record High - $880 per ounce.

Chapter 2

Geordie Girl

The wind howled, and the driving sleet was horizontal on Heaton fields that Sunday morning. On a dark January day, there was no direct land between Newcastle and the North Pole. The poor bairns, kids of just twelve years were battling it out between Byker and Wallsend boys. Football was their religion, it was the basis for all life within their schools, their families and their heritage. In the distance was their citadel, St James' Park, the home of Newcastle United F. C. and all self-respecting Geordies.

Geordies to all and sundry British fold were a race apart, huge communities at the west and east end of the city packed into terraced streets running down to the River Tyne. They were THE people that mined the coal, built the ships and aircraft, and just as important produced the footballers that were the beating heart of Great Britain. To every Geordie, and Maccam for that matter, it was the Southerner that stole their wealth redirecting it into thieving banks, trust funds and corporate institutions run out of London. Football was their game, the part of the world called Tyneside that produced Jackie Milburn, Jack and Bobby Charlton, Gazza and Alan Shearer.

These giants once patrolled the Byker and Heaton fields, in their time carefully observed by the 'Toon' and scouts from far and wide. Jonny Gillespie had the dream that one day he would be spotted. He was cut, almost quarried from a rough part of 60's Byker before "the two up, two downs" would be obliterated to give way to the concrete jungle estates that were all too quickly replacing the tight-knit communities of Byker and Walker. His Dad worked at the nearby shipyards, the world famous 'Swan Hunter' as a riveter, still a methodical manual back-breaking labour of necessity.

The one release was watching his boy play every Sunday for Byker Under 13s. Jonny was fast, tricky and elusive enough to build up a local reputation as a lad for the future. His real skill was building up a close link and 'footie' understanding with his centre-forward in supplying the crosses and the pullbacks for an amazingly brilliant player who never missed the net. It was the centre-striker that was two footed like Bobby Charlton and could fearlessly head the heavy laced-up leather balls like 'wor Jackie Milburn. It was this touch goal scorer who above anyone else in the Byker Boys group that was tipped to go all the way and do it for the Toon one day.

Only 5 feet 2 inches tall, with a short pageboy hair style, the striker boasted already a pair of sturdy powerful limbs, the tools of the trade. Sometimes, like on this very day, he sported a tightly fit bobble hat, naturally black and white in colour. The trouble was he was not a he, that protégé striker was a she!

Ange Bramley was different. Like Jonny she was one of three kids with two elder brothers. Unlike the pair and her strike partner, she had passed the 11-plus examination and made the grade to the local girls' grammar school. It was almost certain that Jonny and her two brothers would waste their schooldays and end up leaving with no academic qualifications, to work in the shipyards.

Not only did Ange have a future in an ambitious grammar school, but she was also able on Sundays to pursue her real passion, to play football. Needless to say, in 60s Newcastle, there were no organised girls' teams. Nevertheless, her Dad Raymond had plans for her! He had spent hours, days, years, at first recognising her two footed skills and then perfecting them in their street of cobblestones. As her first coach, he was lucky as Kimberly Street was a kind of cul-de-sac with a bricked-up wall at one end.

The local boys had chalked up a replica football goal at the centre of this wall which made for great shooting practice with the kerbs of the street acting as the perimeter of their pitch. Many World Cup 'finals' were played out on this small patch of cobbles, not to mention a few broken windows.

The boys and Ange would get together to play games with the new white plastic balls that Raymond as coach of Byker Boys could supply. At first, the lads got Ange to ref the games, then occasionally and begrudgingly placed her by the wall as 'stick' goalie. No boy ever wanted to be so stuck and restricted as stick, so they would only ever play that position as "rush" goalie, the modern-day equivalent of the libero sweeper!

Ange gradually worked her way from down the street at No. 10 where the girls got together to play "Hopscotch" (a paving stone mobility game popular at the time) to the prestigious label of "Rush Goalie". What the boys didn't expect from her at the age of 12 was her fantastic ball skills. In short, she could score goals at the other end whilst being "Rush Goalie". As boys do anywhere in the world, they were not going to stand for that. They resorted to violence and foul play to stop her.

Every evening before dark, she would come home, beaten up and bruised. The boys were never apologetic. If she wanted to play with the lads, she had to play by their rules. Their patch was carless, no one in Kimberly Street could afford a car! The only danger in this street came from the delinquents that took pleasure out of "chopping" the likes of Jonny and Ange. However, it was just a matter of time before the boys warmed to Ange Bramley. She never cursed or complained at the treatment being handed out. She would take the knocks and hand out a bit of stick herself. In a funny sort of way, she had completed her street credentials, indeed she was to push the boat out even further.

Ange deliberately would get home early from school and get out of her school uniform to don her Newcastle United strip, all male gear she got for Christmas from her Dad. In those days, girls just never wore shorts, but Ange didn't give a toss. On went the bobble hat, plastic ball in hand, she would slam the ball against the wall and try and control the rebound, tricky skill off the cobbled street stone. At first, her initial shot was with the right with the left foot control, then the left foot shot with right control off the rebound.

Her favourite was volleying the ball at the wall, a sort of "Keepy-Uppy" exercise with only one foot. She would at first establish a record number of volleys with the right without the ball landing on the ground, then try and beat the record with the left. She loved it because she invented the self-styled game. As the boys arrived, they would marvel at her skills.

Soon enough the boys were won over as she would introduce them to another game, using the street kerbs as a 1-2 'wall' pass and then shoot first time at the chalked wall-goal. Both kerbs would be used to ensure left and right foot accuracy. They looked and learned, and now they were to do the one thing that no other group had done on Tyneside. They wrote a note to Ange's Dad to ask him to approach the Byker Boys' Manager, Jim Stadden, to include Ange in the Byker team.

"A girl in Byker Boys, no chance," was his reply. Jim had been a staff sergeant in Montgomery's Desert Rats, a stickler for team and individual discipline and appearance. His father had been a player for Sunderland and in all his days he had never countenanced women playing the National game.

"What is the world coming to, man?" he replied to Ray at the local King's Arms late one December night.

"Look Jimmy, just give her a try. On New Year's Day you always have a kickabout on Heaton Moor with the lads, have a look at her, she's no prim and prissy woossie with long black locks, she even looks like a boy at her age."

"Alright, just this once, but even if she was good enough, d'you think the League would allow it, her playing?"

Ray looked with stern intent back at the army man and reassured him that it would be possible with both parents' consent. He knew them, it would be a tall order, but he did have some influence because he was on the referees' panel.

The next stage was the easy one. "Blimey, the girl can play," Jimmy decided, and within days she was up there at Centre-forward alongside Jonny, a pairing that would wreak havoc amongst the junior teams from North Shields to the Team Valley. Within the Byker team, they were to be nicknamed "Bonnie and Clyde", and between them in the second half of that 64-65 season scored 36 goals in just 12 matches.

* * * * *

Squadron Leader 'Joe' Messer had retired from the Air Force and was awarded the OBE for his heroic services in the Defence of the Realm at the Battle of Britain. He was inseparable from his beloved Spitfire; short and stocky with a croaky, deep voice, he led groups of inexperienced pilots to glory and lifelong injuries. He had seen it all, the long and the short and the tall.

He had settled in Gosforth to enjoy a retirement from the RAF mainly raising a son and a daughter, the quiet life but relishing the sport of hockey. His wife and daughter had been introduced to the sport on Tyneside which was nurtured by a minority of enthusiasts, mainly in the Girls' Schools. His daughter, Susan, was to play in a Newcastle Schools' Tournament that very Saturday and she begged her Dad to come and watch on the side-lines. Susan was a defender of note and had been selected for Northumberland Girls, so there was expectation in the air for her school to win the Tourney for Newcastle Girls' High.

They reached the final that day, a full day's hockey with 30-minute matches played on Benwell Sports Centre's new redgrass/shale pitch. She faced a team from across Newcastle in the East of the City and she openly wondered how a team from that part of town could ever get to the final. They had never done before.

She was soon to find out! In just the first fifteen minutes her opposing Centre-forward had scored a hattrick with the Eastenders going on to win 5-0. Susan had never played against such skill at pace with unstoppable shooting, as she sought solace from her 'Squadron Leader' on the touchline. Joe equally was curious to know about this player that had vanquished his pride and joy. He approached the opposing team's teacher and asked her in congratulation, "who was that whirlwind of a Centre-Forward?"

"Good ain't she, her name is Ange Bramley."

* * * * *

Joe peered down that very night at his black shiny new telephone and dialled a number deep in the heart of Somerset. After a great deal of clicking, the operator duly connected him, "Is that you, Boss, it has been a long time, it's the Squadron Leader here, how the devil are you?"

"Always a pleasure, Joe, I'm fine. Where are you these days, up north yes?"

Joe continued as the two former combatants exchanged pleasantries. Then suddenly the Air Force man came out with it, "Boss, I have a girl here for you, she's special, I have never seen a hockey player like her at the age of 12. She has GB star written all over her, but her parents are poor in terms of money. Please look at her as I know with your backing and what the school can offer, she will go all the way."

"If she's good enough for H.G. Messer, she'll be good enough for me and Millfield School. Can you get her down for half term?" replied Boss.

Little did young Ange Bramley know it then, but she was to be considered for a free place at England's most expensive and prestigious school, headed up by the notorious 'Boss', Jack Meyer of Millfield in Somerset.

'Boss' was Millfield and Millfield was 'Boss'. If Thomas Arnold, the Head of Rugby School, was the forerunner of the British public school system in the 19th Century, it was Jack Meyer who pushed ahead with educational principles and delivery in the 20th. From the start, he was exceptional, a true light blue Corinthian at Cambridge which he followed in the 1930s as a cotton trader in India. His double first-class degree was to come in very handy.

There he developed the more cavalier side of his nature playing zone cricket to the highest level. By 1935, he returned as the governor to six Indian princes who sought after a more tutorial approach to finish their education in England. Yet Jack had been clearly moved by the poverty he witnessed in the teeming masses in and around Bombay. It was this wealth disparity that formed the basis of his educationalist principles as he opened Millfield School in 1935. At first the land was leased from the Quaker family Clark of Street, boasting broad sweeps of the Somerset countryside.

The buildings dotted around the 'Campus' were mainly of Nissen huts, rounded structures of corrugated design from as early as the First World War. Cold and uninviting, they stood in complete contrast to the splendour of Millfield House at the very centre of the new school. So in short, 'Boss' would subsidise the talented poor by increasing the fees of the rich, ultra-rich, from Middle Eastern royalty to the sons and daughters of prominent Westminster politicians to the offspring of top popular music icons.

His staff initially was colourful to say the least. It wasn't that he did not believe in qualified teachers, he just valued more the University of Life, as he attracted company business moguls, professional sportsmen, eccentric artists and musicians, and close associates from the military and commercial world. Timetabling was flexible, but standards were high at all times. He believed in leisure and relaxation time for all as well as he would cancel the school day at 9 am, give the pupils the day off whilst bussing the staff for a day out at nearby Wincanton races. Above all else, 'Boss' was the epitome of risk, the avid gambler!

* * * * *

Meanwhile, back in Byker, Lynn Bramley was parading her protégé up Northumberland Street to find an outfit for the trip south for Ange's interview. She had to look her best, but all the dresses were just beyond her pocket, so she fitted the shy centre striker out with a grey suit top to go with her little grey skirt from her school uniform. Surely with a nice cream blouse that would be formal enough for those southern softies!

Ray had spoken to Ange's Uncle Jack who had recently bought a green Ford Anglia. That popular model was to take the three of them down the 650-mile round trip on pre-motorway England. Ange could not believe how far it was, she had never been south of Gateshead!! The Millfield experience would take a total of three full days.

County after county passed by the fogged-up windows, but the three of them knew they were getting close when south of Bristol, the fields were greener with cattle interspersed with acre after acre of apple trees. They were truly in cider country with Cheddar cheese on every menu. Millfield's long drive up to Millfield House touched on Ange's nerves, but the main emotion was one of bewilderment, what was she indeed doing in a place like this?

It was half term, so the place was empty apart from the hub of operations at the ivy clad house at the end of the drive. Ange was ushered in by the school secretary, slightly uncomfortable in her new 'suit', and with her hair pristine and shiny shoes, she was told to go into the library where 'Boss' would meet and greet her.

She noted amongst all the columns of books, there was a chair and table; she duly sat down and waited. There was an audible murmur from the ceiling. She couldn't make it out and it kind of frightened her. Her eyes picked on a ladder with four rungs up to the top of a bookcase. The nasal soundings were human in tone! Somebody was snoring and as she stood up, she could see a sheet and a pillow with a fully clothed, grey-haired man nestled inside a makeshift bed where two hundred books should have been!

'Boss' never slept, he just took catnaps. He climbed down in an open necked white shirt with grey worsted trousers, "You'll be Miss Bramley, eh? I've heard a lot about you, my dear!" He then burst out in fits of laughter as he finally focussed on Ange's neatly pressed grey suit and disappeared next door into the secretary's office and returned with a gym slip outfit with the Millfield colours of navy, green and red emblazoned across the material. He mused, hadn't Joe told her parents?!

"Get into that lot, and what size gym shoes do you take?"

Ange was mortified! She had been rehearsing in her head all the right answers to any potential questions. More than anything else, she could not expect him to comprehend her strong Geordie tones, but how could she ever be posh?

"Are you ready to go outside?" Boss enquired.

"Why aye man. Howay, man, where we gannin?"

Boss led her to the front lawn where there was a 9-hole putting course. By the first hole was a hockey stick and ball which she picked up with ease. Her task was to weave in and out in numerical order and then back down the spiral as fast as she could. Boss sat glued to the action with a foldaway chair and a stopwatch. She ate up the course to the delight of her father, a distant onlooker whilst her Mum was given a tour of the school by the secretary.

Jack had seen Tony Robinson, the double Olympian on the staff complete this 40-yard slalom and she without doubt was a dead ringer for Tony. He then led the Geordie Girl down to the 100-yard grass sprint 'track', where two fully developed young girls were limbering up. One at 18-years old was the West of England sprint champion, the other a 15-year old already competing on the school's track circuit.

"You will have a 20-yard start on Yvonne and 10 on Gillian," at which point 'Boss' pulled out a gun, a hand pistol to start the sprint. Ange initially startled, nervously took up the crouched starting position, waiting for the gun. She knew she had to beat 'em. Off to a great start, she pulled ahead of Gillian after only 60-years increasing the distance, but the 'Champ' was making headway and agonisingly pipped her on the tape.

Ange trooped back, desperate she hadn't won the race as, for her, second place was always to be last. Jack Meyer now sidled her across to a football goal, where the Bristol City Under 16s schoolboy goalkeeper was awaiting the girl with the funny accent. She was to have three penalties with Ray anxiously looking on. Ange was brought down to Millfield as an athletic hockey prospect, but Ray knew something now that even Jack Meyer was unaware of.

"Come on, bonnie lass, show 'em what you can do," he mumbled.

Ange, never having heard of Bristol City, placed the first two penalties bottom right to the keeper's left glove. Easy enough, now for the third. All her eyes, her balance and her feet pointed to a repeat performance. "Bristol City" bought the dummy flinging himself to the ground to the same corner, only to be humiliated as she had turned her foot over and curved it innocently into the opposite side of the goal!!

'Boss' couldn't control himself, he just burst out laughing. He brought Ray over to him, "I didn't know she was a footballer," he exclaimed.

"Ange, show the Boss what you can do," passing her a dirty old Penny coin.

She tossed it with her hand high in the air, intercepting the downward coin with her right foot cushioning it on her outstretched toes before flipping onto her left foot, and then up to her right thigh holding it there for the return pick up from her Dad.

'Boss' could not believe what he had just seen, and inviting the family in for tea afterwards, quietly took the parents aside and offered Ange a full scholarship. Over the previous five years only Mary Bignall-Rand, who was to go onto Olympic long jump gold, and a promising youngster from the Valleys called Gareth Edwards had achieved such a prestigious honour for rugby.

A month later, Lynn and Ray were still knocking their heads against the brick wall. Ange refused to go. She loved Boss and all he stood for, but now approaching her teenage years she just could not leave the 'Toon', she was Geordie through and through with all her mates in Byker and Heaton, and her love for Newcastle United was a lifelong commitment. It also hadn't gone unnoticed on her father that she was taking a fresh interest in fashion, makeup and music. Her close friends were all 15 and dolled up, they were already regulars at 'The Club A Go Go' on Saturday nights.

"If you send me to Somerset, I'll run away and get back to the Toon," she screamed at her parents, who had no chance at all.

* * * * *

It was five years on and Boss was on his penultimate year. He loved watching the School at Cricket and Rugby, but equally enjoyed the many tournaments that Millfield had been accustomed to host with its formidable array of sporting facilities. That Easter, 1970, was his last winter season and it was a Girls' County Hockey Tournament from all over England. As a man that represented Somerset himself as Cricket captain, he was still keen to see his Millfield girls in the County team produce the winning goods, even more so as he was to present the medals at the end of the Final.

Somerset were getting hammered at this last hurdle by Northumberland. With minutes to go, and down by four goals to nil, he had suddenly recognised what was bugging him all through the game. He had seen that stride length and turn of pace with the ball stuck to the stick somewhere before. He took a pride in discovering talent and then seeing it realised in front of his very own eyes. The striker from up north had walked off with another hattrick of goals.

As she now, a 17-year old starlet, came up to receive her winner's medal from him, he fumbled around in his pockets. He had found what he had kept there for five long years. The other Northumberland girls all received their medals; Ange Bramley, last in the line, was presented with an old 1935 Penny, the one that got away.

Chapter 3

Malibu Shack

"OK, Stevo. Time's up, you're outta here," Dan called the end to another session. Frankly then at 4 am the bartender of the Malibu Bar and Grill was more than worried about one of his regulars this time. He knew that the errant drunk's shack was just along the strip, but the real problem was in the form of his orange soft-top VW Convertible parked in the lot.

That fact alone meant that Steven Faaronheigt was intending a 'burn-up' along PCH to get to his parent's place that night up in Camarillo. The doors slammed shut behind him and within seconds, Stevo was hurtling up the Pacific Coast Highway with the canyon to his right and the glistening moonlit waves of the gentle Pacific to his left. He had done it many times before.

Once he got beyond the boundary of Malibu, he slowed down appreciably as his mind took in the serenity of his situation. He had earned this paradise, an American Dream set on the west coast of daily sun and never-ending evenings either at his 'Shack' or spent partying amongst the beautiful people along the shoreline. He even held down a steady but flexible job at ABC Studios pursuing his professional assets in the entertainment industry that was Los Angeles.

He mused carefully through his alcohol stained brain cells that he had survived. Yes, he had survived Vietnam, that hellhole of killing fields. His two-year draft had not left any physical scars, just the agony of those sounds running through his head even there that night, the helicopters, explosions and more helicopters. Then the 70s had come and gone. Just how he had endured the fallout from South-East Asia and the hippy generation that had sprung up from Haight-Ashbury made him shake his head.

The VW pushed on past Pepperdine, its university stone still visible in the reflected moonlight. His thoughts turned back to the 70s as the radio belted out one of those hour long shows never interrupted by a chattering disc jockey. It was playing non-stop folk-rock. He responded to sounds, his consciousness normally stimulated so often by enhancing agents. Not tonight endless lines of cocaine or taking a specific West Coast 'trip', no he was floating up the highway on cocktails. The Who, Hendrix, Pink Floyd, kept him afloat, then his band (he always referred to them this way) The Grateful Dead pumped out a long, long instrumental track.

They had only partially survived by this early part of the 80s. Heroine overdoses, diabetic comas at worst and jail sentences at least had taken their toll on 'his' Band. Nevertheless, he and Jerry Garcia were still standing, so life was cool. He dreamed awake as 'Neptune's Net', a kind of biker grotto, could be seen up on the right to the continued drones of psychedelia. Without doubt, Stevo was up there as a leader of the 'Deadheads'.

As if by divine intervention, commercials invaded the airwaves almost pushing his foot harder to the metal as he hit the long straight by the 'Net'. There were no cars, just the sound of the waves hitting the shore. He was half way home, his parents' home, beyond were the steep sand dunes of Point Mugu, round the rocky corner where the canyon terminates abruptly to give way to the flatlands of Oxnard County.

Yes, the two of them had also survived. They had left war-torn Europe at the end of WW2, an Austrian engineer of a father married to a feisty mother of Breton heritage. Emigration from the jackboot of the Third Reich was not easy, but Tomas Faaronheigt had very specific skills, he knew how to assemble rockets. The need was there just 60 miles up the coast in these decades that followed the war.

What a life they had experienced in the new dormitory towns spreading north beyond the Valleys into coastal California through Thousand Oaks and onto Ventura and Santa Barbara. Their only worry had been for their son when he picked up his draft papers to fight in Vietnam back in the 60s. For that was why they came to America, to cast away from the dreadful memories of war. Steven was their only child and born in Ventura in 1949, they were banking on a marvellous future for him and their own aspirations in the Sunshine State.

By now, the Beetle, Stevo's only compromise to his Germanic heritage, was just a few short miles from home. He was about to turn the radio off when suddenly a series of tracks from Alan Stivell's À l'Olympia boomed out returning him to full sobriety. His mother would play this Celtic Rock, formed as a true Breton, as her only leaning to modern music. She was very much a concerto lady stuck on Mozart, Brahms and Beethoven.

Stevo's love of the West Coast sounds and Stivell's regional Breton folk vibes played on his Celtic harp to a background of Scottish and Irish jig beats had fostered a fanaticism towards real authentic music. Then in 1983, having spent over 12 years commuting to Burbank as first an outside broadcast cameraman, then onto the studio mixing side attached to ABC's Monday Night Football Presentation, he was intent on developing the connective threads between visuals and audios in the most dynamic of ways.

Earlier in 1980, he had decided to invest in a 1-bedroomed, 4-roomed apartment along the ocean just north of Malibu. It had cost him a fortune, but by then, with a little help from his friends and parents, the 'Shack' was brought into and subsequently changed his world. Physically it was a 'Bar' of a kitchen, an extension from an open planned lounge which backed onto the beach. On the same single floor was a middling size bedroom and a standard size bathroom with relatively high ceilings.

To Steven Faaronheigt it was a quadrophonic main arena with tape and vinyl decks, the kitchen bar was just that, a multi-fridged Bar space, and his bedroom was simply a paid-up homage to 'Jerry and the Grateful Dead'. Posters, record players, LP covers and concert tickets from the Hollywood Bowl to Cornell University's Barton Hall adorned the walls. The bathroom was nothing other than a sound box. When he bought the place he evidently clapped his hands in the high-ceilinged bathroom to review the echo. "That's it, you have a sale." The delighted realtor was just dumbfounded!

'The Shack' was to be his life, both professionally and socially for some time to come. ABC for years had hired out for him a midweek apartment in Woodland Hills just along the valley from the studio in Burbank. He had no necessity for his own pad, but now in his early 30s, he wanted identity, his own space and vibe, away from war memories, the drug-fuelled parties in the Canyons about LA, and before then, the strictly guided existence of growing up in the dormitory town of Camarillo.

Camarillo appeared as quiet as ever. He stepped out of the Beetle, remarking to himself that it was still dark. He had his own key to a bedroom built on the side of the house when he was a teenager. He was to creep in without waking the folks as it was 5.20 am. Loaded earlier with drinks from midnight, he patted himself on the back, he had made it!

As he collapsed into bed he glanced sideways to fathom out a note, "Lunch with Alex at 1 pm – Be ready!?"

It was from his father Tomas, more an order than a kind invitation. Alex Stamatovic was the Secretary of the local Ventura County German Society, a group whose mission included a whole variety of offerings of German culture estranged in California which ranged from films, foods, concerts and evening events naturally conducted in the German language.

Stevo regarded it all as harmless enough, no hidden Nazis here, just gentle folk that held a loyalty to tradition before it was all buried below a sea of McDonalds and K Marts. Anyhow he was always pleased to see Alex, a family friend from the old days of the America Youth Soccer Organisation. Alex was one of the founding fathers in Southern California that attracted just a handful of boys' teams to play regular matches. He had been insistent on his fellow "German" émigré to encourage his son to play on one of the teams.

The Faaronheigts were not natural athletes, but Tomas felt it would be a healthy pursuit for his son, especially as the League placed great emphasis on participation rather than the quest for winning at all costs.

Lunch on a Sunday was always a pleasant affair with Alex, now a Dental Technician by trade comfortably affluent enough to provide a bottle of German wine and an entire Apfelstrudel for dessert. Evidently the two families had built up the custom of the guest supplying a sumptuous final course to the meal.

"How's the soccer going, Alex, it's become really big these days?" enquired an interested Stevo,

"I've had it mit that game (Alex never bothered to use the English word "with"). For some time I have moved to Youth Field Hockey. I'm still administrating and using basically the same approach as we had back in the Valleys in the mid-sixties. Do you still play, Stevo!?"

"No way, two years in the team, then I got drafted and that was it. Hey, field hockey? Thought it was a Preppie game for girls back East?"

Alex, visibly irritated that someone of German (Austrian!) heritage knew so little about the team sport that was to be top of the tree of The Games the following year in LA, listed the major contenders for the medals. West Germany was at the top, of course!!

"What about you, Stevo, still working those cameras on the Monday Night Football?"

Tomas, now slicing up the 'strudel with lashings of cream, interrupted in proudly boasting his boy had moved into the more creative realm of the studios at ABC. He left the detail to Stevo to explain the intricacies of editing, mixing and the final production processes. At this time in early 1983, he had been highlighting a novel idea of comedy where unfortunate accidents involved families with kids, dogs and gardens with water. It was introduced as "Bleeps and Bloopers" and would become world famous in many languages. The interplay of craziness with appropriate musical takes to augment the humour was really Stevo's grand design.

"You should do an Olympic version of it," said Alex adding, "I could put you in touch with the people right at the heart of what is going on in our Field Hockey teams."

"That could work, sensational Alex, that could really be cool. I've always wanted to get involved with the Games in a practical way. If you supply me the guys' names, I'll take it from there."

"Come down to Moorpark any Sunday. There are eight marked out pitches, the guys coaching the kids are all members of the Olympic squad, and the new coach, some British guy is always there. You'll love it, it'll remind you of your Valley days as a soccer striker!!"

Stevo was now on a mission, this was his big chance to get involved with the Olympics. He still had to convince the executives on ABC Sport about an 'Olympics Bleeps and Bloopers' programme, but he knew they wanted to know all things Olympic in 1983 as they were to have full coverage of the Live Event in August '84.

However, before he put things in motion, priorities first, he had to leave his parents' place to head back to "The Shack" where he was undertaking his 'Wall of Sound' creation for his bathroom. Cabinets, mirrors and even the bath itself had to be withdrawn to empty out the room with the high ceiling. It was now to be his voice-over room with only space for a single shower. 'The Box', as he termed it, would still be equipped with speakers and mikes for recordings and to entertain him with his vibes everyday at midday at the showerhead.

His new challenges meant meeting more people with more opportunities to indulge in his other extra-curricular habits. Already he was working flexi-time at ABC, his daily slog commencing at 1 pm and culminating between 8 and 9 in the evenings. Dinner dates were always late and invariably led to liquid aftermaths well into the night.

His nocturnal energies were legendary. The part of Southern California between Santa Monica, Zuma Beach and the bars of Malibu was a magnet for California girls. Instantly accessible off the highway, Zuma was miles long with fine sand equipped with all the formal and informal games you could think of. All ages gravitated to this sun worshippers' mecca, but it was carved into sections or Towers numbered 1 to 14. Each section attracted specific age groups, families, sports enthusiasts, so keen observers like Stevo could target his interest in the type of Babes he would politely meet. It was no accident that the world famous 'Baywatch' TV favourite was filmed right here only 1,200 yards from his apartment.

Time was now rushing by, and 1984 had started well for Stevo. He had not only made himself known through ABC to the IOC as one of the outside broadcasting advisers, but he had also cleverly infiltrated the Men's Field Hockey group. Alex and his cohorts had bought into his ideas to film the players in training extensively. It must be remembered that Field Hockey up until this point was never systematically recorded. Yes, cine-films had covered 1970s World Cups but from a centre line one camera shot, and that was special, that was match play only.

There was no doubt that he had landed in the right place, the right man at the right time. He was first and foremost a cameraman which had yielded to his promotion to the studio to produce edited highlight packages. His relevant experience was well received notably as his "Bleeps and Bloopers" shows had been catapulted into the highest of rankings.

He now was to go for the kill. He recognised early on that the International Body for Hockey, the FIH, did not at that stage have a clue how to market their sport with a more dynamic approach to coverage. In addition, Stevo had struck up close alliances with Alex's management team, and the head coach in particular. All these now could act as vehicles for his ideas which could easily be relayed onto the IOC through the auspices of the ABC.

So, he set out his proposals, following times spent with the head coach perusing hours and hours of hitherto recorded tape from Australia, Holland, India, Pakistan and Britain. Any recorded material collected by the US team on their travels would be rehashed and overdubbed at 'The Shack'. To say that he experimented with material would be putting it mildly as he cut and spliced, labelled with graphics and applied music to the match play sequences.

The problem with Stevo was the harder he worked, the harder he played. Throughout this period, he had been cautioned by the LAPD for a string of traffic offences ranging from driving erratically, to speeding, and rather comically to hosting an excessive number of persons in his convertible (8 girls in his VW). Put it this way, he was well-known to the LAPD as one of the city's excessive playboys and in Tinsel town, that was quite an achievement in this era.

Foot to the metal, he pushed his ideas of, as he put it, "sticking a bit of pizazz into this conservative sport."

Stevo could never understand why the rules cracked down on such a minimal amount of cursing, violence and showmanship. He felt the game was made for it. Hockey had a murderous lethal weapon, a rock-hard ball and two goaltenders that looked like something out of "Star Wars". Unable to convince the authorities that we should have timeouts accompanied by loud West Coast rock music, and equally unsuccessful in his trying to convince the hockey people to legalise stick checking (hacking) before taking on the ball, he relented to the more technical off the field dynamics.

Through the correct channels, he insisted on 5 camera shots, two behind the goals, two low-lying and one centrally placed higher above the action. At the field of play at the dugouts, he insisted on the coaches having headphones. The reason for this was he wanted the cutaway shots to be "verbally active" with coaches cursing at the players, the umpires or at their own assistants in the stands!!

Also, for the coaches, he could produce in a video library form the chosen match for the day's schedule. Any coach in any sport could book a booth for a maximum of two hours from 8 pm onwards on matchday and at any time on rest days the game or event of their choice at the library in the UCLA or USC Villages. This was a welcome first for hockey coaches as they could rely on a very professional 5 camera shoot of the games, and inside the booths, they had access to pause, fast forward and for the first time action replays of the goals, the penalty corners, and what led up to the penalty corners! Note here that this package would not include the two-man commentary teams associated with each match, just the crowd and pitch noises only for enhanced effect.

One Steven Faaranheigt had achieved all that. From his areas of expertise alone, it was said that the coverage of the LA 1984 Games had taken the broadcasting of Field Hockey into a modern dynamic era. Stevo was ecstatic.

As an engineer, he had pulled it all off and apart from his inner circle of friends and lovelies, no one, just no one knew who he was!!

The Circus had come to town, and in an instance it was gone. Yet, the sport of hockey had been pointed towards a new direction and it was the experience of Los Angeles that had made hockey far more aware of itself. How was it to sell itself on the world stage against the competing team sports like American Football, Soccer, Basketball and Rugby? It was no coincidence that LA was heralding in the real era of Astroturf as a surface of recognition of the needs of the players and spectators alike, of commercial sponsorship, and of an inward look at the rules to make the game more attractive to all.

There were luminaries before, but they were nearly all players. How ironic it was that the real personality who ignited the potential for hockey was a figure so contrary to the image of those diehards from the old countries. Imagine a visit from President René Frank or Brigadier Atif of Pakistan to "The Shack" in Malibu!!

For the remainder of '84, despite offers to work in Europe, Stevo celebrated his newly acquired fame, and did he celebrate! As with too many artists, it could be said that it all went to his head and before long he was riding down the same road as Jerry and the Grateful Dead. His alcoholic binges were now to include the additional substances that had given 'The Dead' their bumpy ride over the preceding decade.

Any positive, personal or professional impact at the Olympic Games, the first Olympiad to have made a substantial profit, was to have significant rewards for those involved. Gradually Stevo was mixing more with Hollywood and music moguls and therefore with all the baggage that was entailed in that company. The work hours were cut shorter, the evenings longer and the nights turned too quickly into day. Relationships had become more temporary than ever whilst the number of acquaintances skyrocketed, but the list of true friends was noteworthy by their absence.

Even the detailed experimental work in "The Box" at the Shack diminished with the bedroom a refuge at the end of too many excessive evenings. Stevo was only 35, but when he stared in the mirror, he saw a man of nigh on 50. At ABC his reputation had been established, and though many of the glittering libertines were facing a man in decline, none of them were prepared to help the techno wizard of Malibu.

Now by the middle of the decade, his daily diet of pills, uppers and downers, stiff brandy cocktails and harder drugs were pushing him over the edge. He knew it, but what could he do at this stage?

Stevo needed to take a sabbatical from work, so he handed in his notice in September 1985. His view was to escape from all that came with work, the pressures and the parties, and regain sanity to his life. The only environment he could achieve that calm was up in Camarillo, to return to the quiet stable presence of his parents and away from the cauldron of Los Angeles.

He would take a few days to tidy up 'The Shack' and take in some long hours in the sun on a liquid diet of mineral water and orange juice. Then early on the Saturday evening, he packed his suitcase on to the backseat and climbed into his trusted convertible to head up the highway for home.

The miles disappeared so quickly behind him, he had that familiar feel of freedom. After all, he deserved everything that California had given him. He was to resurrect his career and a new lifestyle. All the images of his adult life flashed before him as he was blinded by the setting sun. For two short seconds he never clocked the motorbike pulling out of "Neptune's Net" parking lot.

Frantically he swerved to avoid the couple on the bike with his car veering into the side ditch in a plume of smoke and flame. The bikers on the veranda witnessed it all before their very eyes, sprinting to pull him clear, but it was too late.

Steven Faaronheigt was slumped over the steering wheel motionless, but the radio was still blaring out a 1960s hit song by Billy Fury. Its title: Halfway to Paradise.

Chapter 4

North and South

Bob Henson had been there many times. The pick-up from New Street Station was a regular part of his workload from this central hub of England's rail system in Birmingham. An old hockey mate had asked him a favour to present himself to a physical training specialist called Alec Masterson. He strode up from the subterranean depths to recognise Bob, a man that had formed his own sports marketing company years before it became fashionable.

The two associates became well acquainted during the ride in Bob's taxi service. They were well aware of each other's credentials having excelled in the burgeoning industry that was sport in the 21st century. In Alec's case, having worked in sports medicine in a small University environment for a decade, he was responsible for producing top level Athletes, football and rugby stars and international cricketers. Henson's 'Route to the Top' organisation had clients that were household names in Track and Field and Tennis.

That morning would be different for the two men as they were venturing into the sport of hockey. Alec had noticed in his outpost that there was a surge of students in the city wearing hockey 'stash', the kit associated with hockey even as leisure wear in the streets and in the lecture theatres.

"Ready for Cannock and the Futures?" asked Bob, as their assignment was to observe the tournament that was England Hockey's shop window for talented Under 18 girls. The Midlands club had a double wet field pitch alongside a four-tiered club pavilion, perfect for the huge assembled gaggle of supporting parents to be England hopefuls.

The contesting teams represented the best from the North, South, East, West and Midlands. Just to get to this level and annual trial, was an achievement in itself at an event which exuded anticipation and enthusiasm.

"He wants us to take the first game between the Saxon Tigers and the Mercian Lynx, the Yellows v the Reds!" Bob exclaimed, perusing the names down the programme.

"No wonder he's not coming 'til this afternoon, he hates all these Aussies and American style nicknames, says the players lose their regional identity", Alec added, knowing his Boss only too well,

"I'm surprised he's coming at all, thinks the women's game is packed out with Tomboys and a breeding ground for Daddy's girls, and don't even mention the other categories", Bob added.

They stood on the high bank for the opening encounter, and just after fifteen minutes, they were drawn to a game within the game. Two girls were standing out like a sore thumb. Alec could see quite a physical battle, whilst Bob was very much appreciating the contrasting skills between that Red No 3 and the Yellow No 8. It was non-stop attack versus defence as the Tiger was pouncing all over the Lynx.

Nevertheless, the Lynx parried all the blows with a timelessness seldom seen of a girl at her tender age. The game ended with honours even but with both girls respectively scoring open and penalty corner goals.

"His Lordship's here, then", Alec noted as his Head Coach had at last arrived during the lunch hour. His four eyes in the stands made a beeline for the man they called 'Mojo', seemingly a shortened version of Monty Jolliffe.

"Eh, Mojo, we've found two gems for you", as Bob pointed out their names and number off the programme.

"Maddie and Michelle, spotted them three years ago, but they're still looking good, yeh? Gotta get down and see their Dads, both of 'em true blue with sport running through their veins. One's a rugger bugger, the other has been a top footballer. Leave 'em to me. Any other worries?"

Monty never really cracked the traditional English language. He didn't give a toss, what with his Dad working down Mother's Pride Bakery in Hammersmith and his Mum a charlady, he did know one thing. That big plus was his ability to get on with the parents from the British working class. He struck rich with Maddie and Michelle's Dads as they had so much in common with the Head Coach.

Maddie's family were gritty northerners who had worked up't mill through the generations. They knew their place, loved their kids but did not indulge them. 'Their sporty daughty' inherited her father's love for the team game, and what came difficult for all her contemporaries, was simply easy for her. Mojo had witnessed her timing and reading of the play which equivocated to a 21-year old, and that was when she was in the Midlands Under 14 team. Anything to connect with weighting of the passes and positional awareness, no coach needed to teach her.

Yet, there was a shyness, an inbuilt modesty about her person and it seemed she only spoke when she was spoken to, which to some came across as aloofness. She did not seem to communicate a great deal on or off the pitch but would rather do her damage in the shadows.

Michelle was at the opposite Pole. Brash, extrovert, already fully developed physically at seventeen, she demanded everyone's attentions by her actions. These could be followed up by words, but only as subtle reinforcements. Unlike Maddie's education at the 'local Comp', Michelle had already lucked out with a scholarship to an all-girls private, independent school. As a player, she did excel in the special skills, which in her mind, put her above the mere levels of standard attainment of her team mates. In short, she was a match winner, and at school, every season in every team, Michelle was the 'go to' player.

Whereas Maddie was content in her withdrawn nature, Michelle was the hub of the group, charming to all who crossed her path. Both girls had been blessed with such stable family units that had evolved from blue collar roots into very comfortable support systems. Their work ethic through the generations was not lost on their daughters either.

Mojo duly thanked Bob and Alec for their efforts that day with the customary pie and a pint at the local hostelry, the Clubhouse bar. They would list their other stand-out girls for the day, but the Head Coach was only mildly interested. His support staff knew why!

"So d'ya think they'll move up to our little corner of Britain?" asked Alec of his boss.

"Dunno, yet, but confidential lads, I see them as a pair, you can build a whole team around the two of them, remember like the two Bobbies, Moore and Charlton. Personally speaking, those nerds of England Hockey should be building the full England team around them for some time to come. Promise me something, I will, however, approach them separately. Mum's the word!"

Contrary to the Coach's cynicism, England Under 18s did select the two Ms. From that point on, they were to be the target of every self-respecting hockey university in the land, and notably those 'red carpet' colleges that were the so-called Performance Centres. The Baker's boy from 'Ammersmiff had always steered his training and coaching of kids and adults within the big city centres, and certainly never to the dictates of Milton Keynes or Marlow in Buckinghamshire or any other bleedin' shire!

Nevertheless, he tackled the two Ms as they were to play in Junior internationals home and abroad. His stingy college would never stump up expenses, but Beeston in Notts was not too far to observe. Nor was Germany! He followed the pair everywhere as this age group team yielded top results with Michelle on the scoresheet regularly. Mojo even watched the Squad's warm-ups, noting body language and compliance to the team and individual choices of activities before the games.

Whereas Michelle was out there in the front with the group of more outward oriented players, Maddie just tucked in at the back seemingly uninterested in the group model. In the back of his mind, was the importance of compatibility between the two divergent talents. They had to converge, and sooner or later if they were to figure into his plans, he might need to ask some potentially awkward questions.

Then the bombshell! Even though both England girls had informed Mojo through their fathers that they had placed his seat of learning at the top of their UCAS (British University Applications) list, their appeal merited an even bigger threat, from American Colleges. Since 2005, there had been an increasingly steady drift of applications from English female hockey players to further their studies in America's very differing and challenging environments. Naturally, the financial implications were very favourable with these newly acquired open scholarships to young women that had previously been dominated by male athletes for football, basketball and track and field athletes.

The talk at this time amongst the young England girls that had already been picked for the Junior National teams, and Michelle and Maddie were in that bracket, was that here was an opportunity for a lifetime, what, with all the facilities, and concentration on their chosen sport for three hours a day for four years. Only Loughborough, Birmingham and Durham could possibly compete with that.

England Hockey could not get their heads around this 'brain drain'. For some time, they had witnessed some of their best talent slip away across the Atlantic and at regular intervals. Susie Rowe, Xantha Travlos, Harriet Tibble, Becky Dru and Sarah Mansfield with many others had taken the risk to clear out of the England 'Single System' to seek academic and sporting success in the United States. The risk was founded on solid ground as England's governing body incredibly sent out threatening letters to all Junior players stating that the girls would not be considered for further selection if they took the American educational option.

They were proved to be true to their word, as the five girls mentioned above were never given a chance to play in the Senior teams of the future. It was alright for young women to spend seasons in Holland, Belgium or Germany, but the USA was taboo.

American collegiate recruitment was legendary. Their budgets just for travel, hotels and expenses ran into the high five figures in searching out the appropriate talent. There were even specific agents conveniently based in Europe to act as scouts, even though this was technically contrary to NCAA rules, to recommend emerging players in Britain and on the continent of Europe. After all, these were the 'star' players earning up to $40,000 scholarships a year known as the 'free or full ride'. Schools like Connecticut, Virginia and Maryland by winning NCAA titles were not mucking about, they were looking for the top performers, and where they came from, money talked.

Hence, their approach to Michelle and Maddie. That summer before the start of the Academic year was to prove a testing time for Mojo and his staff. There were high level meetings between him and the school staff, parents and even the girls themselves. The only group that were left out of the picture were England Hockey, but ironically, they were in a difficult position too. They could not afford to lose these girls to America for four years, but almost equally they were loath to allow them to pursue their studies in Britain away from the designated 'chosen ones' of Loughborough, Bath and Birmingham.

The argument that won the day, of course, was the girls' individual and independent education. Both had expressly applied to Mojo's abode for essentially two reasons. Firstly, the scope of the reputation of the Course they had applied for, and secondly, the man himself. He was a thorn in the side of the authorities who with scant resources, produced players and teams of outstanding merit. There was one common thread between the two very different kinds of girls, and that was independently they wanted to play with a smile on their faces. Even though one was outstanding, and the other a top goal-scorer at the age group levels, they both harboured a disdain, almost disaffection to how the game was presented by a succession of schoolteachers at the England group level. Whereas England's management had limited, adopted schools' personnel for their coaching, Holland had Lisanne Lejeune and Tom Van T'Hek, over 500 Test appearances between them for world-winning Dutch teams.

The two girls were looking for fun and personality in the University set-up along with real individual advancement. They did not feel that atmosphere in either the American or within the English Single System and thus, avoided them.

By September Mojo breathed a sigh of relief, as all his new recruits walked the walk into his office for one-to-one interviews before setting off for the University's pre-season training camp down in Devon. This was an annual good opportunity to take in the new recruits' aspirations and ambitions whilst giving the players a full understanding of the University hockey environment which was to be their central core attraction for three years.

Maddie knocked softly on the door. Mojo began with,

"Ideal season for you last year, how'd you enjoy the England group?"

After some hesitation with eyes directed away from her future Coach, she rattled out her reply,

"I didn't."

"What d'ya mean? Playing for England, a young girl's dream."

"Not for me, they treated you all like peas in a pod. You had to play in their pre-ordained manner, to their predetermined system, backed by training on pre-established skills."

"I see," said the Coach, immediately recognising that Maddie was indeed a thinker beyond the average! After all, she was to study psychology in a high-powered Department.

"They keep on hassling my Dad, to get me down to their Performance Days, but I've told them I am not available for England, and that's that. My priorities lie with my course and our hockey team here at the University," she insisted.

"Don't fret, Maddie, I understand, I feel certain you're gonna have a great three years up here. By the way, we believe in winning. Are you with us?"

"You bet!" she broke into a broad grin for the first time.

Next up, a few minutes later, Michelle literally bounced into the room, all wiles and smiles. It was clear she liked this Coach ever since their first meeting at the affluent club in London she knew as her first hockey home. Laughter and *double entendres* filled the air as they engaged in conversation from London's best concert venues to her amazing summer vacation spent as a hotel 'trainee' in the South of France. Hardly a thing on hockey!

He thought what a handful she was going to be for everyone, hoping mostly for the future long-suffering opposition. She never stopped, boasting that she had wangled a prized single room in College as a fresher. That was unheard of in this University's experience.

"How did you manage that?" he mused.

"I told them I suffered from periodic bouts of insomnia which was not what a potential roomie wanted to hear."

Single room, thought the Coach imagining what her real game was about! She just winked at him!

"Michelle, you know they want you down at England training assessment days, don't you? You scored a shed-load of goals for them last season."

"Coach, I am not the slightest bit interested. England Hockey is not for me, I have other ambitions up here and one of them is to win the BUCS Title for you, me and the team."

Well, that was that then. He just could not believe two girls of such contrasting backgrounds and temperaments could arrive at the same conclusion, without any prompting from him, of all people.

As Michelle turned away with a customary wave, he had already decided that during their tenure at university, the British University Challenge Cup was his and theirs for the taking!!

The girls settled into University life as all 19-year olds would do with a sense of wonderment at facing so many new aspects to life. For the first time, they were in charge of their own affairs with Michelle making full use of her independent quarters, whilst Maddie was pleased to be sharing with a fellow psychologist. Money was not really a problem for either of them for they had both worked their summer passage, so it would only be the 'Dad bank' for strict emergencies.

As expected, they tore into their training three evenings a week. From the outset, Monty had placed the two in core positions as Maddie would control the back area whilst Michelle had the task of opening up opposing defences from an attacking midfield. He was very wise to appoint a no-nonsense captain from a big family of younger brothers and sisters. Whatever Monty might think and diligently prepare off the field, the triumvirate of girls were going to run this squad for the next two seasons on the field of play.

The captain, Fran, knew she had a job on with the two internationals, but she had developed a very close relationship with Monty the previous year, and trust was the centre of their understanding. They had quiet Friday late afternoon meetings where nothing was hidden. At the first she brought up a perspective that 'The Mojo' could not possibly have noted as it concerned the team socials and the interaction of the first team players.

Call it feminine intuition, but in the early weeks she had got the impression that the 'two stars' were not on speaking terms. Both were active in their own right to group activities, but there was a lack of eye contact between them and seldom, if not ever, did they address the squad as "we" or "us" as former England team mates.

The months ticked by with tremendous results, notably at national club level. Monty and Fran continued their meetings with the coach taking the lead in reinforcing Fran's early impressions. Maddie and Michelle just did not attempt to relate. There was no direct antagonism there, but Fran again insisted that with two such outstanding players in the team, the other girls would start to gravitate to their individual of choice. This trend was not as sinister as it sounds now as like personalities always tended to herd together. A potential divide was ready to crack open.

Yet Michelle was the queen of the local nightclub scene with the team's more vivacious characters. She already had clapped her eyes on a 2nd year student, who certainly looked like Beckham and thought he played like Beckham. He was still attached to Charlton Athletics' policy of retaining players on a part-time basis whilst at university. They became such an item that before long Michelle, let it be said that she did have a cultured southern accent, was nicknamed 'Posh', with her beau inevitably named 'Becks'.

All this was over the top to Maddie whose main focus outside hockey was her academic performance. Her friends, mainly female, were more likely to attend theatrical productions and an array of student society gatherings, which abounded at the University.

The months rolled on into the second season after a record-breaking year. With Michelle and Maddie, there was great interest from the England Under 21 group, but again Mojo, to his frustration, had to decline on the girls' behalf. It was, simply put, a stalemate.

Internally, he would call management meetings with Fran at the helm with now her two vice-captains, but it was stark noticeable that there was only one time when all four attended. He blamed himself for letting the situation drift, but frankly chickened out in fear that he might upset the two starlets.

His squad was now getting stronger as girls were much more likely to attend Universities achieving league and student competitive success with England juniors at the helm. The stigma of choosing a University outside of the England Hockey performance centres was starting to evaporate, but the rumours circulated that in the next Olympics cycle after the London Games, strict residential centralised enforcement around Bisham Abbey, would be the norm.

"I told you so, Mojo. You wouldn't believe me, it's like Stalag 39 down there. So many of my mates just do not want to know. We all want a life of our own, not to be owned by Sport England and UK Sport," said Michelle at a team social.

It was now the third year, and the good news was that Fran had decided to continue her education to read for a PGCE with a solid aim to teach thereafter. She had had plenty of practice over the previous two years and certainly had become an expert in behavioural observation. The team had matured into a stable unit with outstanding contributions all round as Monty and herself had broadened the team's effectiveness by not depending upon the twin talents of Michelle and Maddie.

For the girls it was a dream come true when they lifted the National title for the first time in the University's history. Their hockey was enterprising and delivered with the joy of playing in a style that excited players, coaches and spectators alike. Mojo was beside himself on 'Finals' Day, a man crowned as a coaching icon as he achieved team success without one single representative player. He had so much to thank Fran for with her balanced, stabilising role and her dedication to the team cause.

He had left the undercurrent alone. For the entire three years it mystified him about the two England girls, surely something had happened in the past? Was it while on England duty? Then he thought back to that distant day at Cannock.

Alec had described the pair as "having a right ding-dong! A battle for supremacy in their part of the field." Monty Joliffe had put a lid on whatever it was, and it was his relationship with Fran that had really won the day.

Nine months after graduating, the University held its Alumni Sports Day when all the Old Girls and Old Boys returned to take on the current teams in "The Champagne Challenge". Mojo always loved this day. For him it was the time to feel the gratitude of past students for all the care and expertise he had given to their hockey progression. He simply was written into their individual life stories.

The Head Coach was ecstatic to see Michelle and Maddie were attending the day and he could not wait to discover how well they had taken on their hockey careers. They had left as champions and the hockey world would surely welcome them back then as adults into the national and Olympic scene. His hopes were high.

The Alumni team lined up before the start, but there was no Michelle! Where was she? Then Mojo spotted her in the crowd, limping around with 'Becks' by her side. She was in a cast.

"What happened, Posh?"

"Did it playing football, torn ligaments in the ankle."

"Football!! What about your Hockey?"

"Nah, gave it up after graduation, Mojo. Becks introduced me to the Women's section of his club, Hendon FC. I just love playing at weekends away from my City Banker's job."

Monty was distraught at Michelle's news as he entered the post-match cocktail party. Everyone was all dolled up when he made a bee-line for Maddie.

"How's life and hockey, Maddie? Back in the National eye?"

"Hi, Monty, great to see you. No, I have moved on from hockey, you'll be sad to know I am emigrating to New Zealand," shocking Monty to the core. He needed a drink.

His desperate thirst was immediately answered by a short dark-haired friend of Maddie's, carrying three glasses.

"Let me introduce you to my wife, Monty. Her name is Tina."

Chapter 5

A Canterbury Tale

Where once he had strutted, he now was shuffling. The dishevelled sexagenarian struggled to carry his prized possessions in three plastic bags along the crowded lanes of Chaucer's Cathedral City. He heard little, as frequently the noise of the backboard and the frantic applause of the crowded stadia still rang in his ears. Yet there was something about the way he dodged and sidestepped oncoming youths with their headsets that suggested the elusive ghosts from the past were still very much part of him.

To those students he was surplus to requirements, a man that had lost his way with trousers dangling around his lower posterior and trainers that more resembled beach flats. A long plastic anorak nearly covered both as if to hide this shabby mobile wardrobe. A bright young teenager glimpsed a weathered face of reddened cheeks with what looked to her like damaged pot marks around a mouth with chipped front teeth.

She stared now into the eyes, and to her bewilderment, he responded with a smile and a sharpness of the turned eye uncharacteristic of a senior citizen. Even her uninterested air recognised that here was a man with a past, a past that clearly extended beyond this walled city of Christendom.

His movement continued apace with a hint of a limp, surely a reflection not of recent trauma but of lifelong scar tissue. His appointment for the day was a rummage around his favourite charity shop followed by another Super McDonalds filler for lunch. As he ordered another Big Mac and fries, he reluctantly peered down at his expanding midriff and convinced himself he still had an uninterrupted view of his toes. No way, the express ready meals had taken their toll over the years of indulgence in cheap, easily accessible grub.

Suddenly he crossed the road, more to avoid a former inmate of a council-supplied four bedroomed property in the Forrester Close neighbourhood. A community dependent upon conflict, drugs, mental breakdowns, but most of all, on the state benefit system known as the Thursday wage packet. It was a Thursday afternoon and our pensioner recognised a fellow beneficiary that enjoyed preying on other recipient's bonus payments. He had been beaten up before, but during this vulnerable period he had learned to work the British system well, and that involved lying very low in cardboard boxes in open stairways or in church external recesses, night or day.

Living on the streets, semi-homeless now for five years, meant he adopted a streetwise mentality to find and exploit space, and to maximise his opportunities when presented. His earlier life of a differing setting had trained him well in those skills. Some would even say he had been one of the best in this sceptred isle at doing just that.

Gradually he had adopted his new lifestyle in his kind of town; Canterbury was his patch, and penniless as he was, he had described his daily grind as 'feral'. He had devoted his attentions between a rundown shelter from the council one month, then the streets the next. Any coins he had were spent on the snooker hall, the charity outlets and Wetherspoons serving the cheapest cider in town. From 2011 onwards, this was his existence.

Before then he had relied on the benevolence of a host of sporting friends, those former associates that took him in almost on a Bed and Breakfast basis while he looked for that temporary refuge from the turmoil that had dominated his life for nigh on a decade. The trouble was that his idea of temporary often was very much at odds with how his hosts defined temporary.

Those hockey heroes had done their best to keep our senior alive and kicking. The warm blanket of the city's Hockey Club protected him, offering bar roles and coaching responsibilities within one of England's biggest and most ambitious hockey institutions. Too much time spent behind the bar resulted in an easy temptation to drink more and more, as he could sometimes see that he was, despite his more settled life, on the margins of life in a club that boasted a great deal of success and affluence.

What had he done to deserve this living hell for fifteen years? Who else had been affected by his apparent demise? And how had hockey played a prominent part in his fall from grace?

Ronald Herbert (a.k.a. "Roly" or "Golly") Brookeman was born one of seven children, the son of a bookies runner, and a ballet dancing mother from Camberwell in South London. His father's profession led him to the doors of the Masonic Lodge. Roly was the son of a Mason, but very early in his life, he lost his father to an untimely and premature death.

This inadvertently enabled his bereaved mother the chance to send her elder children to the Independent School of Royal Masonic. If you are a believer that we are all determined by our genes, it would be a wee bit ironic that Roly would develop from a runner and a dancer, both attributes involved heavily with the sport and entertainment industry.

He was a child star. Whatever he turned his attention to, be it cricket, football, hockey, he had a natural command of the skills and the athletic movements required to go all the way to the top. Many of his contemporaries also had those assets, but Roly was different. He entertained, as he played with a smile and mischievous giggle never far away. More than this, he brought a sense of fun to all around him.

For those a little older who read these pages, he preceded Paul "Gazza" Gascoigne and was a Stan Bowles, Tony Currie and Gazza all rolled into one. He loved the movies, any form of eccentricity in terms of dress and speech which he could mimic. He was a watcher of people whether you were Roger Self, the Great Britain Olympic Manager, Tommy Cooper the comedian or the cockney groundsman. Once observed, Roly could be any of 'em. In this earlier era, personalities were actively included in our top club and national teams. Today, forget it, no room at the inn.

Nevertheless, he could play. His turn of speed, change of direction with the ball have never been equalled by any Englishman since. His wide range of hand and ball skills were just made for a right hand side forward. Was he reliable on the field? Do me a favour, but this lack of predictability surely made him more effective, a nightmare for defenders from London to Lahore.

Yes he was an individual in a team sport, but he built up a series of formidable pairings on right side attack with 'Doc' Thomson, Mike Corby, then David Westcott, all world class midfielders. Roly would bellow, "to my stick", or expect your vision to be spot on to meet his perfectly timed run. Track back? In yer dreams, he was the player with the ball.

Naturally he found England and GB selection automatic from 1973 to 1982 at all levels and acquired gold medals at European club level with Southgate. Playing alongside him was not just a privilege for all of us, but it was also therapeutic. There was no such thing as a 'downer' when Roly Brookeman was around!!

On a long 747 excursion with England, suddenly there was a commotion at the front of the aircraft with excited screams amongst a gangway filled with raised voices. What was going on? At least a dozen children were gathered around some kind of special event with stewardesses struggling to keep control. It was Roly's muppet show! He had a range of popular puppets from his bag, including Kermit the Frog and Miss Piggy.

His mimicry astounded all around as the kids bayed for more dialogue between all the puppets he brought to the show! Roly's England teammates did not know whether to laugh or cry!!

Then, in the Semi-final of the Nehru Tournament in Delhi, England were to face the then World Champions in 1977 in front of a partisan 20,000 crowd. The two captains, Bernie Cotton and Govendra jogged up to the centre line for the toss to start the game. The England captain was presented as a gift from the sponsors with a 6-foot hockey stick. It was an amazing piece of art from Chakravarti.

Bernie jogged off towards the England bench to hand it over for safekeeps, but on his way Roly Brookeman intercepted him as he was already in his position to start the Test at right striker. The opening whistle blew, and all hell let loose as the crowd swelled into a rapturous response. Roly had thrown his own personal stick onto the side lines and played the first minute of the game with the 6-foot Chakravarti!!

Back from that famous tour of India with the medical journals eager to interview all the squad on the joys and perils of touring an entire subcontinent, Roly Brookeman had to settle down a bit. Luckily for him, he made up a blind date and was to meet his future partner and wife, Fiona. For his career which would extend internationally until 1982, she backed him to the hilt. Once this dedicated journey in the hockey world was finished, it only seemed right that they would move on together in marriage and to new horizons.

Although he reached two European club golds with Southgate, the years that followed 1978 were fallow in achievement. For the second time, politics had interfered with Great Britain's entry to the Olympics. After the Kenyan late withdrawal and boycott in 1976, necessitating a first reserve Britain to miss out, now it was the British government's turn with the western world in agreement, to pull out of the Moscow Games because of the Soviet's invasion of Afghanistan.

Roly, with many others from his hockey generation had been the victims, their dream of Olympic glory dashed from circumstances beyond their control. He never, never forgot it. It was too bitter a pill to swallow. Then when England's World Cup team plummeted to the 9th/10th play off at the World Cup in '82, Roly had had enough. Too many of his contemporaries had retired early in

1978 or 1980 for personal or professional reasons. To lose the talents of Long, Aldridge, Owen, Featherstone, Thomson and Saini during this period, and not one of them had reached their 28th birthday yet, was a reflection of what a mess England and British hockey was in at this stage. Roly's mates had all gone!

Thus, in 1982, Brookeman's career was over. What, apart from returning to his teaching job near Slough, could he do? He faced that rocky road that follows the committed athlete after retiring from top level competition. He cemented his relationship with Fiona who rightly had plans for the two of them. She was forging ahead with her job at Wilkinson Sword, and surely he would respond with a committed approach to full-time employment.

He did, and he didn't! He was offered a part-time role under John Cadman, the then Director of Coaching, with responsibility for South-east England. However, was this what Fiona had anticipated after his international days were over? The salary for a start was meagre and it pushed Roly back into hockey and a part time mentality. They had married in 1982, and there were many friends and associates around them that were concerned that Roly was drifting as coaching at this stage in hockey's evolution was an experimental occupation outside of school teaching.

From his individual standpoint, was Roly's personality broad enough, analytical enough to take on team coaching? Yes, there was no doubt with the likes of John Cadman and David Whitaker, and also his contemporaries at Loughborough, Mike Hamilton and Paul Sorensen. These men were thinkers in the game that had given them a structural and organised approach to team performance.

Roly came from a differing angle. Maybe his form of attention to individual detail along with a manner that could inspire individual flair really might take on, but many of his closest allies had their doubts.

One of those had to be Fiona. She had stood by him for seven years and still there was not enough certainty in an uncertain 80s world. Then, as so often happens, lady luck shone her light on the couple. Roly Brookeman was offered a full-time role at a top independent school, at St Edmund's in Canterbury in 1985. Like many of its rivals, the school boasted a fabulous location with views above the cathedral down in the city, tremendous sports fields, solid academic status and real prospects for a career in the teaching, coaching and pastoral side of education. He had landed on his feet, and Fiona was equally delighted now at their prospects.

Canterbury was also a hockey city with an ambitious hockey club, soon to be one of the founder members of the National League. Roly could pursue his interests at club level, but they were to play second fiddle in these years as the career at St Edmund's and his family were his only priority. Along came two children in 1987 and 1989, as Fiona and Roly settled into family life. With stability and Fiona's support as mother and wife, they flourished in family and friends' circles, building up a solid entourage of close associates in and out of hockey in what was one of England's friendliest cities. Their social life was very much the bedrock of their relationships whilst their children were growing up.

By the new century, school roles within his department and the pastoral House system meant that the family was fully ensconced in the St Edmund's way of life, which paralleled up with Kent College, King's School, and a host of other famous schools in the city. Their friends were very much in the same situation as life in boarding schools unfolded. In all these careers, fringe benefits abound in terms of accommodation, holidays and indeed, in the general prestige that their profession carried in such a tight environment. In short, they were holding down jobs for life.

Yet, one must always wonder whether this line of solid predictability was positioned to the mould of Roly's personality. To his way of thinking, he was giving it a full shot, but there were others that noticed he was not the type to grind out the years, which in turn would not reward him with the levels of status of his yesteryears.

He just could not rid himself of post-playing career syndrome. There he was, now a steady Eddie with defining responsibilities of marriage, children and school. As a player, those regular areas of life were looked after by the managerial coach, club officers and the hockey overlords. They all just wanted Roly to perform and become centre stage as the star player, the one that was heralded by newspapers and magazines every week.

Roly had tried hard for nearly twenty five years, twenty of them as a married man with Fiona. As with all relationships, strains were becoming apparent and pressures built up, escalating between the couple. The detailed background has to be within the context of the couple, but suffice to say that it led to the subsequent explosion that would leave a great impact on the future lives of Fiona, the two children and the immediate family and friends.

St Edmund's was a tightknit community of a boarding school that always left little to hide. Talk amongst the children, in the staff room, in the Governors' remit and within the parental umbrella all played a significant part in defining the daily fabric of those types of independent school in 2002.

It started exactly that way as talk and then suspicion, leading to a major number in the school taking sides. Roly was deemed to be involved emotionally with a specific pupil and although it was not lawfully an illegal liaison, he was nevertheless three times her age. Up and down the land, this type of relationship has been sung about, written about and indeed experienced by a great number of teachers and pupils. It happens. Yet that can never be of any solace to those immediately affected, those family members of both parties. It turns former friends into at least ringside debaters on the rights and wrongs of each individual case, setting them against each other. The damage can last a lifetime.

The relationship continued and was adjudged as inappropriate by the school's hierarchy, and Roly honourably resigned from this private institution in a private manner. Almost as night follows day, his marriage folded, and Fiona and he were separated. It took some time for divorce proceedings to be finalised with the mother taking charge of the children. Roly Brookeman had basically lost it all. The tangible assets, property and belongings were gone, but inevitably the children and his accessibility to them hit him hard. After all, they were the victims of the situation at a teenage stage, a stage that Roly must have known was critical to their future.

Fiona did remarry, and the children did eventually settle into Canterbury life, but only they know how much of a struggle it would have been for them. As for Roly, he at 56 years of age would have to rebuild his life, and as he has been depicted earlier, he merged into another way of survival, because that's what it was to be. His viewpoint that since 2007, his friends rallied round him at first, notably some of the prominent players and officials at Canterbury Hockey Club. Then in real terms, they attempted to bring him in part-time employment as he himself tried to reorient himself as a supply teacher in the state system. Remember he had been married for over twenty years and teaching in the independent sector for seventeen years rising to Head of Physical Education and Housemaster at St Edmund's.

He just could not adapt. The increasing bureaucratic nature of modern teaching with its political correctness and health and safety regulations at every turn was anathema to him. Allied to this, what he perceived as a serious lack of discipline and behavioural control in Kent state schools, sent him in the opposite direction, to state dependency. It did not help when he glanced sideways, to note that his former close associates focussed on their headships and deputy headmaster jobs, were stating to drift away from him. They did not disown him, but when he tried to pick up some extra income by a small modicum of coaching at nearby Ashford HC, it was the end of Roly Brookeman and Canterbury HC. Even his photograph alongside his old mate, the legendary Sean Kerly, was taken down by the club.

He was and remains essentially homeless. Fault is not in the remit of these writings. Yet there lingers that edge, that true feeling that those closest to a troubled soul should always step in to avert a potential crisis, that even National Governing Bodies could somehow be a safety net to protect their former players that have given so much or provided so much pleasure at the peak of their powers. We all loved them when they were great, but after, if they fall from grace, we wring our hands of the matter. Are we not to be forgiven for just one drastic error in our lives?

Roly drifted back to the streets, a celebrated figure amongst publicans and the fellow itinerants he cultivated right through to today. There were rays of hope for him, a journey to Spain to pick up some Paddle Tennis coaching he had qualified for. Then, of late, conducting an open interview on homelessness for regional television, he was at last for a short moment under the lights again.

Then when a former international team mate came to visit him, the sparkle returned, the glint in the eye, the encyclopaedic memory of the glory days returned as if it was just yesterday. Invitations flowed to meet his mates for a city centre drink, as Canterbury was a kind place for alcohol consumption.

His pal was called Rob, a smoker and drinker and also a former professional person now hitting hard times. Roly turned to his old Centre-back wishing him farewell as he took to the open courtyard for another dose of nicotine, leaving his guest with his friend Rob.

Rob had another way of saying goodbye;

"Cheers, mate, you couldn't lend us a tenner could ya?"

The Folkestone International Hockey Festival

request the pleasure of the company of

Mr. Lav Pavlovich   Team Yugoslavia

at a Reception in honour of the Visiting Teams to be held at Motel Burstin, Folkestone, on

Friday, 8th April, 1979

Dress - Lounge Suits   8.30 - 10 p. m.

R.S.V.P.
MRS. N MIROY,
ELM LAWN,
LALEHAM-ON-THAMES,
MIDDLESEX TW18 2TD   PLEASE BRING THIS INVITATION WITH YOU

Lav hits the decadent West.

Lav and Judy's hotel dream on the Leas seafront at Folkestone;
The Easter home for Festival teams.

Above and Below: All that glittered was gold for Lav in the Transvaal

Ange's Tyneside neighbourhood.

Millfield, Britain's most prestigious sporting school.

Biker paradise on Stevo's Pacific Coast Highway.

Malibu playground for Faaronheigt.

England's 1978 World Cup Squad
(Roly ringed).

Still a personality in 2018!

Roly's adopted city – Canterbury.

Magreth outstanding at the Berlin Indoor World Cup.

Oasis in the Desert - The Dome in Swakopmund.

Chapter 6

Oasis in the Desert

Teddy Carter had devoted his life to the English public school. Educated himself in private institutions, he devoured the classical upbringing of the upper echelons of British society. He was a prefect, house captain and took up similar positions up at his Cambridge college where his sporting talents pushed him into the welcoming arms of hockey.

Never a competitive type, he represented in his decades of teaching and coaching a rather untypical lighter side gaining a sincere popularity with boys and staff alike. His local Sussex hockey club was singularly unambitious playing in the lower leagues of the South. Many a time he was recommended to take county, club and representative teams but he always resisted the temptation of committing time outside his dedicated teaching duties.

By profession, he was a geographer, a non-smoker and strictly single, ever since the College gardener had run off with the love of his life at the age of 21. He enjoyed the female company when it presented itself at boarding school dinners and within the strict code of his academic friendships but that was it. Regarded by all as an affable confirmed bachelor, he drifted through just two public schools throughout his long career.

Yet he never lost contact with his one sporting passion, that of hockey. Old boys came and went with a regular supply of county players and the odd international who swore blind by his teaching methods and coaching influence. They would return to their alma mater, teasing him about his obsession about "tracking".

"Tracking" was the term he used for disappearing out of the comfortable English environment each summer to experience another culture or way of life. For two months in July and August, he would abandon creature comforts for backpacking travel to just one country, coexisting between Spartan accommodations and questionable modes of transport. He only had one rule and that was his chosen nation had to belong to the worldwide hockey community!

So over the three decades of the 80s, 90s and noughties, he had accumulated tracking trips to the Soviet Union, Chile, New Zealand,

Zimbabwe, India and Japan to name but a few. His remit was to see the country on the wild side and to inculcate himself into the national psyche of sport, and hockey in particular. Over a period of twenty years of such activity, Teddy had been proposed to three times, offered jobs in national governments, being beaten up twice, and only deported once!

His motives, he would say, were very much misunderstood! Now, in 2017, he had settled for the soft life and taken early retirement. His teaching pension would go far, allied to inheritance assets he had accrued from his family. Teddy remained fit throughout his life, never taken a pill or a fizzy drink with the only visit to a doctor being confined to a few Friday evening beers with JB at the White Horse in the Sussex village of Storrington.

On retirement he had chosen this charming village amongst the South Downs chalk hills. He loved to walk hills, enjoy the sporting world go by at the local clubs, yet have easy access to the coast only ten miles away. His tracking days were a thing of the past.

It was a mild November morning with the leaves still fully laden on the soft southern trees when the postman delivered a padded envelope marked KLM on the exterior. Thinking it was another publicity promo, he paid it scant attention until he noted the signature, that of a Mr Coen Asges. Teddy checked the postmark; it was from Amstelveen, KLM Headquarters in Holland.

He had known Coen as a club secretary, a friendly fellow from his earlier travels both in Holland and South Africa where Coen was stationed as an operations manager. The letter astounded him. Coen was very clearly instrumental in opening up a new service to Namibia, to Windhoek via KLM. He was in his last year of full-time work and the Dutchman was inviting Teddy to join a small party of hockey mates the following summer to enjoy an African adventure.

'Never say never' went through Teddy's mind. What was particularly attractive about this free business class travel was Coen's declared intention to watch the FIH World Cup Qualifier for Indoor Hockey in a very un-African place called Swakopmund! And all this to celebrate the Dutchman's 60th birthday with a very festive but hockey-mad group of 10 fellow travellers.

For Teddy, it was time to go "tracking" one last time!

The giant Light Blue Bird touched down at Hosea Kutako Airport in Namibia's midwinter. It was 26°C! Teddy had enjoyed Coen's company revisiting former times and getting an outline for the two-week stay. It was to be divided into two parts for the party, a 10-day safari up north, returning via the skeleton coastal dunes, and then taking in the African indoor championships in Swakopmund. The prize, a World Cup placing up for grabs at the Berlin World Cup in 2018.

The Englishman true to form cordially sought permission to meet up later on with the rest of the guys in Swakop. Coen was even more magnanimous in positively claiming no problem there, but also introducing Teddy on their first night at Joe's Beer House to the Namibian Coaching Committee. It was a convivial evening serving up Windhoek lager beer in true German tradition with the whole atmosphere steeped in original colonial artefacts.

Teddy was delighted not only to gain insight into the background and the state of Namibian hockey, but also to be invited as a guest at the forthcoming tournament of the Namibian Hockey Association. He returned to his hotel that night needing to know much, much more about this country which boasted the lowest density of people in the world and its very name moulded from one of the harshest deserts. Note that Teddy's definition of "tracking" was for him to set the sport of hockey within the culture and history of the nation and its surrounding influences. Then to track the development of the sport right down to the latest event or tournament.

Hence, his two days in Windhoek National Library were paramount to the "track". He learned more about "The Scramble for Africa" in the south-west corner where German colonialism clashed with the pastoral economies of the Herero and Nama tribes, indigenous to the land area contested. Following the Herero Wars in the first decade of the 20th century was the discovery of diamonds near to the South African border by the Orange River, inland, and off the coast. The third major element was the apportionment after the First World War to the Union of South Africa under British supervision of the territory of the then South West Africa.

The 'South West' was only to become Namibia in the dying years of the 20th century, and in hockey terms as one of essentially twelve competing provinces within the umbrella of the South African Hockey Association. Teddy had pondered over his two full days at the modern four-storey library that Namibia's journey as a nation, let alone as an FIH accredited hockey country, had been open to a broader set of influences, and many of these were not necessarily convergent.

The very next day the Namibian Association had booked a taxi for him down to Swakopmund on the coast from inland Windhoek. It was the longest taxi drive of all, 225 miles across barren scrub and semi desert, delivered on long straight roads in a bumpy old eight seater driven by Namibia's Michael Schumacher. Teddy was not amused, mainly because he just could not focus on reading at all, whilst Schumacher on the extended line of tarmac would take on the trucks at 150 kilometres an hour. The link road was known across the nation as the Auto Graveyard!!

Swakop appeared out of the coastal mists as the sun set and his trusted driver had achieved his timeline, home for dinner! Teddy had experienced wilderness before, but not like this. The afternoon heat yielded just no people on the journey with just the odd collection of warthogs and ostriches to relieve him of the four hour dry monotony. Yet, here were the distant lights of the 'German' enclave of Swakopmund, a very odd place for a World Cup decider. The morrow would yield a visit to the scene of the crime, the 'Dome' of Swakopmund.

Just 100 yards from the beach stood one of hockey and sports most amazing achievements in the provision for leisure and competition, certainly in the African world. The Dome is huge, imposing as a Premier Sports venue, but is multifaceted as a four-star hotel and conference centre that can host up to 2000 delegates.

More to Teddy's point of interest it accommodates four indoor FIH standard courts which can be transferred to roller hockey, basketball, handball and gymnastics. Out of nowhere in the Desert, came two developers, Paul van Biljon and Horst Fritze, who were determined to create a sporting legacy based on the role that healthy physical pursuits could play in the development of the nation.

With the small but rapidly expanding business and tourist sector fully engaged in supporting the project, the first stones were laid in 2013 with a view to hosting local, regional and international events. Success was the reward for meticulous architectural planning to integrate the variety of sporting and commercial functions. It was indeed an Oasis in the Desert.

Lucky Teddy, as that very morning was to be staged, a Namibian Indoor Women's Team training session. He took up his position at the top of the bleachers and the group of 16 were to train and play internal games just a week before the big event. It had been a long time since he used to play and umpire games indoor at the Crystal Palace National Centre. He never professed to be an expert then on the indoor version of hockey, so here was a chance to fully assess and analyse.

He did not expect much from a nation of hockey girls that nationally could only get to play on two 'Astro' sand pitches outside, and clearly with the exception of the 'Dome', had precious little other than school gyms to perfect their play at the Indoor game.

Teddy was as much intrigued by the player make-up of the group – would they be made up of German descendants, Afrikaans speaking South Africans, the odd British migrant or even of the indigenous tribes of the native country? To his bewilderment, it was a mix led by the Coach, Erwin Handura, who on introduction to Teddy was insistent on any contribution the Englishman could make, would be most welcome!

From that one training session, Teddy had spotted a nugget. He had in all his pastoral and teaching roles never come across a black player of real hockey quality. Yes, of course, with football, basketball, cricket, rugby and a host of other sports too, but not hockey and certainly not a female player. His broad educated line of assessments went out the window as he was mesmerised by her every move with or without the ball. She simply had everything, and to prove it, she took up different playing positions to show she was excellent in her versatility.

He had to meet her. There were three other black girls in the group with some long blonde European exponents that essentially made up the National Indoor team. Towering above them all was Magreth Mengo, the female Pelé. Any observer of team ethics can tell by the body language of the teammates that here was someone to learn from and admire. Yes, she was older, but the most athletic of the group; yet where did she learn her skills and court craft? She dominated every exchange.

Teddy, like an oversized schoolboy in awe of his headmaster, approached "Maggie" after the session. As a courteous Englishman, he introduced himself, and as the captain of Namibia, she was asked where she was from, her home.

"I am Herero, do you know what that is and means?" She affirmed with a friendly smile.

Teddy acted dumb, but was soon to accept that the tribal roots ran deep in the psyche of this modern African woman. She was Herero first, and Namibian second. Yet there was immense pride in her aspect of leading her country, not only as the continent's outstanding player, but as the role model for all her followers of all denominations in Namibia.

For the traditional Englishman this was yet a new world. Indeed, a world apart from his experiences, but he felt empathy with her in a strange way, that both of them had never strayed from their hereditary roots throughout their lifetimes. He was to find out much more about Maggie.

Her father had migrated to play in Soweto back in the 70s for the famous Kaiser Chiefs Football Club led by the celebrated Jomo Somo. Maggie was one of six children with her siblings not really showing any natural sporting inclination. Dad soon realised in taking young Maggie to the local Windhoek School that it was this girl in the family that had inherited his genes. Like so many African sports stars, she was initially an athlete first, tearing up the 400 metre event, but surely sooner or later, there had to be a teacher that noticed her talent?

That teacher was Erwin Handura. More than anyone else he was to play the formative role in her sporting development for many years from teenager through to now at the World Cup Qualifier. Erwin, throughout the 1990s, was at the sharp end of development in terms of the government and coaching association support for young black athletes. Frankie Fredericks had passed through these corridors of attainment, for ten years a World medallist sprinter, so with the right application, Erwin's protégé's journey down after school to Windhoek's Union fields, meant the daily sessions in hockey were to go far.

She was a natural free running striker to begin with, and such was her impact at Development Tournaments that she made the National Outdoor team by the age of 16!! And playing at the All Africa Games in Johannesburg. By 2002, she was rewarded by being selected to go as one of Namibia's World Youth Games representatives for the Australia event in 2002. Not just participation on the field, Maggie had to deliver a series of lecture presentations to world viewers to gain awareness of African sport.

At this enormous celebration of sport, it was soon to be one Magreth Mengo, who would be celebrating wildly. During such events, there are always those that are competing or watching from the stands that are on the lookout for natural talent. In recent times, the onlookers can be of an international nature, as cross-border sports exchanges have become commonplace.

In Maggie's case, it was just a small club in central Netherlands that just happened to have someone there that approached her to think about the chance to play in Holland. That small club was Spandersbosch. Of course, there were many hurdles to overcome, notably ones of cultural change as well as the very different type of hockey experience that she was to undertake at such a young age.

Remember here that as she was from a family background set in deep tribal roots, this venture was going to be an enormous wrench, and this was a cross continental risk, both on and off the field.

When she was asked to bring over some initial spending money to cover her costs of a few hundred dollars, she hesitated. It was not to mentally work out the figure in south african rand, no, it was to equivocate the value in the commodity she understood, the value in cattle, her family owned cattle !!

Initially, she was attached to a Dutch hockey family that welcomed her to some domestic duties and incidental work while she adjusted to new styles of hockey and the day-to-day rush of one of the world's densest of populations. Indeed, again note that Namibia as a nation has the lowest density of the world!

Her early successes as a raw, fast wide striker was not only taking her up the league with her new club, but inevitably there were bigger clubs motivated to tempt her away to play at the highest possible level. You may cry out 'poaching' was rife in the competitive Dutch structure but the hierarchy of progression up the clubs was very well established. It was a fact of life.

The club that was increasingly interested in her services was one of the biggest and most ambitious in Dutch, if not in European hockey. The name, Kampong Utrecht, the club that produced such national hockey figures like Paul Litjens, the incomparable Tommy van t'Hek and former men's National team coach and ex-professional footballer, Rob Bianchi.

For her next two seasons, she was to spend four evenings per week under the latter's tutelage, in short to lead the life of a full-time hockey player. Her athleticism had impressed Rob from the very start which in itself was an enormous compliment to her as his reputation as a stringent physical educationalist was renowned throughout Holland.

Yet Bianchi's philosophies ran much deeper as he directly experienced the football era of Johan Cruyff, and had been many times on the receiving end as his semi-pro DWS Amsterdam had to play second fiddle to the East side of the City, the Euro Kings, Ajax of Amsterdam. The all-inclusive nature of total football was translated into hockey terms through Rob by very simple terminology. Try this one for size,

"The ball must always be in the space,"

This reference on transfering the ball from heavy traffic to wider, broader areas of space was the coaching philosophy of the Dutch. Yet, it was still vital to have players at the end of the space that thrilled to the thought of the one versus one encounter with no defensive cover.

This was where Maggie came in as her raw talent of utilising wide one-on-one situations was paramount to Kampong's eventual success. However, that was assuming she made the starting line-up, as in her first year at Kampong, she sat bench for long periods, often only to be let loose on the opposition in the later stages when fatigue was taking hold of defenders.

It was on the training field where she was to develop the more ambitious stick skills that was to set her apart from her native Namibians for years to come. Speed was a huge asset but it had to be harnessed with attention to detail on lateral movement in individual ball control. In effect, Rob had to sometimes slow her down to achieve real team possibilities as change of direction movements and accelerating in gears was a priority.

Maggie's work with Rob on the training ground paid dividends in the succeeding seasons as Kampong were regularly positioned at the high end in the Hofdklasse, both in indoor and outdoor hockey.

It was not only on the field where Maggie's potential was to be realised. Kampong as a club had the resources to offer her the whole deal where she had the run of an apartment and a club car, but she also had enrolled in a college education, specialising in commerce and business. This was a long-term investment for her as her life was to unfold once she returned permanently to Namibia. She almost for this period in her life, existed positively as a Dutch citizen.

When asked about the culture, the diet and the lifestyle of such a contrasting country, she inevitably prompted up some early adjustments, but everything became comfortable and easy for her except for one notable feature, the weather! She could, despite the warm hospitality of the host club, never get used to the cold weather. Even in balmy October and April, she was known for wearing gloves and an incredible number of layers!! She could never wait for the Indoor season to begin in early December.

Perhaps it was the Indoor arena where she did, and was to excel the most. Her Dutch adventure was to end after several years as she was now entering her peak years as a hockey player. She would wave goodbye to the Netherlands, always grateful for the apprenticeship she had received there and the friends for life she had made in, as Rob Bianchi would put it, "hockey's global village".

Reality of employment, family and national ties would kick in and she would return to her homeland with one outdoor, sand filled synthetic pitch and no Dome; yet to be constructed in 2013. It was simply, chalk and cheese. It was just to be the Africa dimension that was to keep her busy in the coming years.

To many hockey followers, it was a question of where was Namibia? And did they play hockey? After total Independence in 1991, this diamond-rich nation split from South Africa's provincial system and finally had to make their own way in the sporting world. Led by former international umpire Marc Nel and the coaching and development skills of Conrad Wessels and Erwin Handura, lack of government funding was a great hindrance, notably when one focuses on the costs of flights and international events, even within Africa.

Players like Maggie during this last decade were really dependent for their progress in the national game on International and FIH decisions handed down to Africa as a continent. Even when these deliberations were favourable to awarding tournaments, it was commonplace within the continent for countries invited to not even pitch up at the event. The reason? Always cost, money, or political oversights held sway.

Thus, all this eventually did was to reinforce Egypt and South Africa as the continent's power players. How could Maggie and Namibia break this monotony year in, year out? She at least now was committed to domestic sport, whilst the young talent in Namibia understandably looked to South African universities for established and greater variety in course studies.

Hence, by 2017, Namibia was beset by a series of limitations which our triumvirate of coaching administrators had to endure before entering teams to the Africa qualifier for the Indoor World Cup.

Leading from the front, Maggie's girls put these all to one side to beat South Africa (the men had narrowly lost 2–1 in the other All-Africa Final). The hockey community and sporting press were jubilant, asking if this was to be her 'swan song', the opportunity to take Namibia into the Top 10 in a World Cup of twelve competing nations? This from a country with less than 200 regular indoor adult players!

The girls had just finished their last pre-tournament practice session at the Max Schmeling Indoor Stadium in what formerly was East Berlin. The team bus was only 50 metres from the entrance but the Namibian team sprinted like Frankie Fredericks to combat the early morning temperature of -2° Centigrade. February in Windhoek was at 32°C!! They were very quickly on the bus!!

FIH tournament hockey often supports a distinct lack of spectators, but not so for Indoor hockey and definitely not so in Germany. After all, they had pioneered this exciting spectacle as a nationally competitive sport for nigh on six decades.

A week in Berlin was to pass very quickly as the world of hockey was to witness the unexpected skills of the Namibians. Needless to say, that yet again Ms Mengo was outstanding in pushing the players to draw against Australia and Russia and thus qualify for the 9th/10th place final to play ... the United States of America!

Maggie had found a new protégé to play alongside her, a Namibian 16-year-old to repeat her captain's achievement all those years ago. This Windhoek goal machine finished as top goal scorer for the entire tournament with nine goals was called Kiana-Che Cormack. On so many occasions Maggie would burst through from the back to link up with the Windhoek schoolgirl to cause havoc amongst these big 'continental' opponents.

The USA play-off was watched by over 9000 spectators. It was going to be hard for the Americans to deny the African Queens. They were just too determined and too damned good to be deflected from their aspiration to break into the Top 10.

The final hooter sounded, and to rapturous applause, Namibia had beaten the mighty USA. The German crowd was as ecstatic as if it was their own team out there performing that way.

The girls naturally ran a disjointed lap of honour saluting a hardy bunch of 50 jubilant countrymen and women in the stands. Maggie waved and waved ;

was this really to be her last tournament after 16 years at the game through heat and snow?

Then, out of the corner of her eye, she spotted something incredible in the second row of the stands. She had never expected this. A lone hockey fan stepped forward to hand her a large white envelope with an accompanying huge grin. It read,

To Maggie,
Namibia's Oasis in the Desert
From Teddy, the Tracker!!

Chapter 7

England's No. 7

Neil Mallett, the International Marketing Manager of Grays was wondering why he had to journey across the English Midlands to spend a frozen, snowy Sunday with his cousin, Trevor. It was a once a year family duty, but he still looked forward to seeing his old mate as it was usually a very festive occasion. The former Grays man had retired after the Rio Olympics to attempt to enjoy all the areas of life he had missed out on after a quarter of a century of dedicated service to Grays, and in particular to hockey players worldwide.

Trevor welcomed Neil at the door and the kettle was on! All the pleasantries occupied their first hour together. Then by mid-afternoon the host suggested a trip to the Bretton Ice Rink to catch the home side, Peterborough Phantoms, entertain the Invicta Dynamos in the semi-professional National League South, the second/third tier under the English Elite League.

"Don't worry Neil, we will watch it from comfortable seats behind the glass at one end of the Rink. I have season tickets and although it's not quite prawn and cucumber sandwiches at Man United, we do have a spacious bar and buffet."

The Grays Pro nodded gratefully and was full of anticipation to see exactly what hockey on ice could offer. Inevitably, his knowledge had extended to USA v USSR battles, the National Hockey League with burgers, dogs and beer, and the regular scrapping punch-ups associated with the sport. Seriously, he had been thankful for the intervention in terms of goalkeeper protective equipment that ice hockey had passed down to his Grays Empire at great commercial value. Apart from that, he knew zilch apart from what Trevor was outlining before the first 'period'.

He watched intently. Here was a former English International searching out for himself the intricacies of a parallel team sport. Yes, Neil had to be entertained, but more important to him was to gain a true understanding, to fathom out the skills and movement to a pattern of how the game ticked. Were there stars? Were there personalities and core players that controlled the puck and the ice?

"That Number 7 can play a bit, his stick handling is exceptional. Shame he's getting clouted and pinned to the boards, but blimey, he's good. You've got a programme, Trev, what's his name?"

Trevor perused the list of 22 skaters for Invicta Dynamos, as it puzzled him they had only brought a squad of 15.

"His name is Jackson, there's one for your scrapbook, Ashley Jackson!"

Neil rocked back in his chair, he grabbed the programme out of his cousin's hands. He knew it was true, there it was, Ashley Jackson, No 7, his favourite number. It was ten years previous to this icy night that Neil Mallett had offered the then green behind the ears, Ashley, a professional sponsorship contract to use Grays Hockey sticks, Field Hockey sticks.

He knew that Jackson had moved on to Ice Hockey, but he thought it was the Pro Elite League with a concentration of top Russians, Canadians and Americans, and the last he heard was that he had joined ambitious club, the Basingstoke Bison. Still, it re-motivated him to watch this contest to gauge how much progress Ash had made at the game on ice. The former Great Britain star had many of the traits of his turf hockey career as he spent the three periods attempting to unlock the Phantom's rear guard.

His control and change of gear and direction skills were even recognisable on the ice, but more to the point, Neil was pleased to see that his former protégé was really into it, obsessed by the play and action around him. This, despite only fielding a two-thirds squad kept the Dynamos in the game until the last 5-minutes when the Phantoms ran out 4-2 winners. The Dynamos were given a grand reception by the home crowd of 500, and Jacko waved his appreciation to those poor souls of spectators on a freezing January evening. Then it was back, to Gillingham, hopefully by midnight.

Trevor edged his way out of the car park ahead of the local traffic with the conversation switching to ice hockey, the Phantoms and how a GB Olympian of world renown would be preferring the South Division of this League to his fame within international hockey.

Neil was rather nonplussed as well, responding with a thoughtful but mischievous silence. He knew his cousin was an ice-hockey nut, and as he himself had not seen Ashley since the Rio Olympics in 2016, he made a suggestion,

"How about the two of us going down to see him? Can't put the expenses onto Grays anymore, but I'm sure I'll find the pennies to foot three lunches?"

What an idea, Trevor thought, as he was equally keen to find out about the new lifestyle of Ashley Jackson in a more relaxed environment than from the benches of Bretton's ice rink. Neil duly made the relevant arrangements with Ash, who kindly invited the pair a week later to the London Golf Club and its extensive course in North-West Kent. Neil would do the chat, and Trevor would jot down a few lines.

Ashley Jackson was introduced to a pair of ice skates at the age of two years old. His grand-dad and uncle had been instructed in all this as part of their involvement with the sport of players that in those early days were based at the Romford Ice Rink. It is worth noting that there had been a surge in interest in the sport of Ice Dance soon after the Gold Medals of Torvill and Dean around the Winter Olympics of 1984 in the figure skating event. Ash was born in 1987! At the time, there was also television space for club ice hockey at national level with "Grandstand" regularly covering clashes between Wembley Tigers, the Fife Flyers, the Durham Wasps and the Sheffield Steelers in the ten team National League.

By the age of 14, the Jacksons took off to the ice hockey cauldron of Canada. He had continued to skate and be introduced to the sport of junior Ice Hockey. The family enrolled him on some camps at the Toronto Maple Leafs, and despite impressing, there were two elements that were to slow down his early enthusiasm for ice hockey. There was always a suspicion that at 5ft 7ins and a slim frame that he may just be overpowered in the more physical game of ice hockey. The other development was that Ash was to gain a place at Sutton Valence, a rural independent school in the spacious grounds of the "Garden of England" Kent countryside. More to the point, they specialised in Field Hockey.

Blessed with oodles of talent, Ash moved rapidly through the ranks of hockey, and once identified, he was to belong from his first appearance with the England Under 21s in 2005, to that unique breed of being a full-time hockey professional. Of course, there were many before, but Ash was stamped as 21st century hockey man because he was retained by Sport England, UK Sport and England Hockey.

Neil tells the story, "As part of my marketing manager role at Grays I was over in Holland attending the junior hockey world cup in Rotterdam 2005, specifically "talent spotting" young players from all over the world, that I would initially watch play and would then target them to use our hockey sticks - if I felt that they were the right type of profile to shape the next generation of Grays sponsored players.

The England team were involved in a game against a vibrant Egyptian junior team and after a lack lustre opening spell found themselves on the verge of a major upset finding themselves 2 goals down just before half time. At the time I recall thinking to myself that this will take something a little different to spark a comeback. I then began to take notice of a fresh faced young player who was on the field in the left striker role - somewhat unusually for England a skilful ball player, capable of beating an opponent with his stick dexterity and ball control rather than the normal hard running doing a "role" type player. It was immediately obvious, to me at least, that this young forward was a cut above his teammates. Mostly starved of the ball by his teammates passing the ball to him, he then created and scored a goal out of nothing to get his team back in the game on the way to a face saving draw."

In these early years, more enticements were to come his way through the endorsement of Grays, and the newly found riches of a small number of English clubs. Jackson grew up in his formative years as a rewarded sportsman with his every move, and he was worth it as he had developed his skill towards the sharp end of the game. By his second Olympics in London, a PR bonanza for him, as British Hockey fans were looking for a talisman to celebrate our national advance as only one of just five or six countries worldwide to take on full-time contracts.

Neil Mallett now made his big move to substantially push Ashley to a more prolonged association with Grays. He signed up through to Rio with a substantially increased annual award. That was one side of the coin only, as Ashley was to work very closely with Neil on creating the exact mould required for the post 2008 Ashley Jackson 7 Composite Hockey stick. You only have to spend a short time with him to see how much importance he attaches to the technology of his individual stick. Put simply, he is a perfectionist.

Neil recalls the time, "On signing for the Grays brand, we initially set about working together not just on Ashley using one of the current range of hockey sticks , but worked together on a special shape and model where he felt not only fully engaged in the process of creating but was personally emotionally attached to.

As our working relationship and trust evolved, we talked regularly about all aspects of hockey stick design, his views on stick weight, balance, likes and dislikes, as well as his head shape and bow-shape concepts - at a time when the FIH officials were continually doing their best to limit his prowess by altering the hockey stick criteria several times during the period.

As one of the world's creative midfield players and penalty corner specialists, Ashley drew on his up to date on field involvement, and I had years of practical factory based hockey stick manufacturing design and experience to pull it altogether and make it happen. The process involved us both in the creation of a new jumbo blade profile shape that was designed to combine his drag flick requirement of his game as well as allowing his exceptional dribbling skills to flourish. The design and colour combination of the new AJ7 model also resulted in an immediate on field identity linking Ashley and the brand.

I soon began to realise and recognise that he set equally high demands on expectations when it came to his hockey sticks as he did on the field with his own game - to a level unlike any other player I had worked with over the years."

It will surprise no one that his stick model has sold more since 2008 than any other individual stick. Neil Mallett could retire a happy man!

The three diners settled down to eat with Ashley tucking into an extended breakfast of scrambled eggs and smoked salmon. They were surrounded by portraits of prestigious members and the household names of such an exclusive club. Neil began to outline his own association with top level golf now he was retired, while at the same time showing interest in Ashley's established handicap. You've already guessed – he plays off scratch!

Jackson's abilities have been clear for all to see. Timing, hand speed, deception and ultimate experience in the short game have often masked the hours he has spent repetitively mastering his set piece methodology at the drag flick at penalty corners. This intensity of practice on an individual merit coupled with the strain and injuries that accompany that level of single minded application has often exposed him to envious criticism from his detractors of a self-motivated and egocentric outlook on the game.

His team achievements from 2012 to 2014 include a semi-final status at Olympic and World Cup level. Does he have to respond?! Yet fans and coaches always wanted more from him, to such an extent that the reader may require a thorough assessment from an objective former England player and Olympic coach. Well, that would be the writer here.

Ashley Jackson has been the victim of his own success. Up until the London Olympics he really was the property of 'Big Brother' with his every move monitored within a system that required him to be attached or near to the hub of the operations, Bisham Abbey. It was clear that the man's looser connection to that Centre would be intensified after London. In context, it is essential to note which sports were the real winners and benefactors of the 2012 success.

They were not the team sports who had fulfilled their promise, but the individual sports where you had to go from A to B as fast as you could and with as quick a recovery before the next me v you race. The training methods for cycling, rowing and swimming were anatomically and medically advanced down to the least resistant clothing for the event and the technology of the boats and cycles in detailed construction.

Sport England/UK had outmanoeuvred its Olympic competition, and now after 2012, the gurus of this special world demanded to push their method across the remaining Olympic sports. Now the team sports like hockey would be hijacked by sports science where ordinary players stressed to physical capacity could "do the job" for the group non-stop for seventy minutes. The FIH rules of unlimited substitution played into the hands of the laboratory scientists whereby maximum or even extended lines of performance by the support players was guaranteed.

How did this affect Jackson? It did in many ways. First of all, with the new 4-year cycle, he had evolved not only into a world class player, but more pertinently at this stage into one of England and GB's senior players. The scientists and lamentably the hockey management were destined to brainwash even him. In his conversations with Neil and Trevor he came out with two very contradictory statements.

"I know that if I can be at the peak of my game, I will influence the results positively by my individual play."

Now contrast that with this,

"If you pit eleven technical players with eleven tried and tested athletes, there can only be one winner. These days the recovery of the 'beaten' player is immediate, whether individual or collective."

Tragically, one of Britain's greatest technicians has evolved to think this way. He genuinely believed there would be no Dwyer, Shahbaz or Pilay in today's hockey and on a lighter note admitted that there was no longer any room for the ice hockey 'enforcer', the hatchet men spoiling for altercation unless their heart monitors proved their case!

Jackson was lucky! He was in demand, and it was from an unexpected source, the purest of hockey destinations, India. After an experimental low-key stab at a new 'world' competition within India soon after London which was a partial success, by 2013 with approval by the FIH and the support of big sponsors within the country, the India Hockey League was born.

The franchises would number up to eight and play their specific matches in regional centres very much along the lines of the Indian Cricket League. The Indian Hockey Federation could attract the spectator gate money whilst the commercial advertising for the sponsors would be regularly displayed through TV screening. The League would only last six weeks in January and February where there was a hole in the international match play. Indian officials would invite selected players around the globe and there would be a bidding war for their services along the lines of American college players delved out to the Pro Football club drafts.

From the playing side, Indian Hockey would supply 70 or 80, with foreign, the best of foreign players making up the other half in numbers. India had a ready-made preparation programme for their senior and under 21 squads, but so did Australia ominously who conveniently organised a pre-League Test Series before distributing as many as 25 players into the League franchises. Players from Germany, South Africa, New Zealand, Malaysia and early on Belgium and Holland were numerous as both older, near to retirement men and young under 23 up and comings also competed.

Ashley Jackson, with only Lewers, Dixon, Gleghorne and Middleton as British team mates, fetched the biggest fee. For him, it was a reinforcement of his star quality above all his contemporaries and only Furste of Germany and Dwyer of Australia commanded greater fees.

More relevant than the cash incentives was that the Indian Hockey League was a flight to freedom for Ashley. Good crowds, media attention and playing alongside the top Indians and Aussies for him was the chance to excel and enjoy. It was a natural break of playing to his capacity away from the drudgery of weightlifting, power runs and heart monitors. Ironically, he was having a taste of what hockey used to be, and in the home of the beautiful game.

Ashley began his Indian journey in 2013 with the Ranchi Rhinos who won the tournament and the following year gained the bronze. Let me give you the thoughts of a friend in hockey, Mahendra Singh who is now coach to the Indian men's World Cup team, who was asked to take up the reins with the newly named Ranchi Rays.

"The Ranchi Rays was formed from my home state and I had as co-owners none other than the Sahara Group. Ashley was nominated for the FIH player of the year in 2014, so I had followed his progress quite closely before taking up the appointment in 2015 with the Rays. We were to work together, and he was central to planning the team strategy, composition and game plan.

"He was loved and respected by all the team members which included two international team captains in Barry Middleton of England and Manpreet Singh of India along with Aussies, Fergus Kavanagh and Tyler Lovell. Ash always led from the front, be it in training or match play, with his exceptional ability to motivate the players around him. We were crowned champions, he was voted the most valuable player of the tournament and the highest goal scorer with 12 goals. He was deservedly showered with praise by teammates and spectators alike. Ranchi Rays had many good contributions from the core group of players, but Ashley was the fulcrum. He never shirked his responsibility and always put his hand up when it mattered most. May his tribe increase!!"

* * * * *

Trevor and Neil had drunk far too much coffee at the Golf Club and needed a natural break. They had shown Mahendra's message to Ashley before departing to the luxury of the Golf Club men's room. Whilst there, Trevor engaged Neil immediately,

"You know, I noticed something about this lad, did you see his face light up and the positive use of his hands when we were conversing about ice hockey?"

"Yeah, and did you notice how he responded to the note from Mahendra? Sheer joy and fond memories," retorted Neil.

They re-joined Ashley to continue their discussion on India. The England star now 30 years of age in 2018, had explained that the four 'seasons' in India were not a cake walk with plentiful examples of dreadful hotels and food that was variable. Although he had not suffered from contractual complications, he did know that several players had been frustrated by non-payment, part payment or late payment of fees.

Without doubt, the note that struck a chord to Neil Mallett with reference to Mahendra's comments was "his exceptional ability to motivate the players around him." So, in the context of both the Invicta Dynamos and far away Ranchi Rays, the renowned individualist of English hockey was truly a team ambassador that did inspire his fellow players to greater ends.

"I think the England Hockey management have missed a trick here. Put Ashley in an enjoyable environment, he not only rises to the occasion, but influences other personalities in the team." Neil concluded.

This reporter is inclined to agree about his growing maturity. One excellent former South African captain and Olympian used to retort before big games, "This match is not a duty, hockey is a stage, go out now and perform on it."

This line was meant for Ashley, as for him, like Corby, Taylor and Kerly before him, they all yearned for the theatre of the hockey game. Britain's most renowned individual players had this streak running through them, and by the lead-in to the calamitous men's showing in Rio in 2016, Ashley Jackson had experienced this other side of hockey, the crowd, the fame and the financial rewards.

The England Hockey equation of a solid, moderate majority to "do their jobs", with the additional dependence on the flair players from India in Jackson, Lewers and Middleton was to horribly backfire in the first-round elimination of the Olympics. The aforementioned players in the sixteen months before Rio had played in two, two-month India Hockey Leagues, a European Cup, a tour of Australia, two Champion Trophies alongside their club commitments at home and in Europe. Quality had been sacrificed for quantity.

Ash, Barry and Iain had unknowingly been the authors of their own destiny, as had the dozens of Aussie IHL players who also dramatically bombed in Rio. Tough it is for these contracted stars to accept that missing from the Indian Hockey League in 2016 were the players from two nations... Argentina and Belgium, the eventual gold and silver Olympic medallists. To balance the triad of competitive requirements, play, rest and train, was clearly a bridge too far for the professional hockey planners from GB and Australia's mens teams in 2016.

The tragic consequence for this lack of planning in Britain was to blame and make the Indian Hockey League participants the fall guys for the failure where it mattered most. Both with Iain Lewers and Ashley Jackson in the aftermath, it seemed for differing reasons that they were not to play in the future, whilst Barry Middleton at the age of 33 survived to live another day, just.

Ashley was "carrying injuries", "not given a definitive role", "looked unfit", "no more smiles from Ash"; all the quotes come to the fore. He had had enough, so he decided to make the move to his former mistress, ice hockey at the tender age of 29. England and GB hockey had mishandled one of the greatest talents in arguably both Jackson and Lewers, but Ash was adamant, and in conversation with Neil and Trev had revealed some penetrative thoughts.

He described how with the ongoing years he had yearned for the smaller game, whether it be indoor or ice hockey, where there were inbuilt rest periods during the encounters. He was facing up to reality that the big open spaces of the 11 a side game were not there anymore as they were patrolled by the full time aerobic specialists whose ability to recover was never ending.

Would Ashley ever come back to the hard slog of eleven months a year training and playing? Did he have to face the reality of group weight training on a daily basis? Did he just need a break from field hockey after an overloaded programme?

There were many questions buzzing around in the members' room that lunch time at the relaxed London Golf Club. Ashley Jackson, England's finest, had taken a deep look into his soul and his future in hockey.

Wasn't it time for Sport UK and England Hockey to do just the same?

Chapter 8

The Reverend Blue

"You better not wimp out on us, Tone; one more win and the title's in the bag," exclaimed the England U18 Centre-half.

"Don't norr, Gav, me shoulder's killing me," replied his trusted Left Half, a Yorkshireman and proud of it!

"Sawt 'im out Norm, you're from up Norf." So, it was left to the future hockey legend, Norman Hughes at the tender age of 18 to get Tony Porter ready for the Home Countries final game versus Wales.

Norman, away from the team manager, Cim Jones, concocted a 1 v 1 fitness test where he would take a dive to the floor after being tackled by Tony. Norman, flat out, peered up to witness Tony's Karachi King stick, his defensive weapon, with a sticker on the shaft's face, stating "Jesus loves you!"

It was rumoured at the time that the future Bishop of Sherwood thought about diving into a confession box to confess his 'con'. Not at all, at this stage Tony Porter was committed to the sport of hockey.

A bright lad, Tony worked his way through Hertford College, Oxford, registering an undergraduate degree and an Oxford Blue, playing in the same team in 1972 as Brian Belchers, the captain of South Africa, the brilliant GB Olympian Rui Saldanha and the most memorable of them all, Selwyn Maister, the New Zealand Gold Olympian.

Tony was heading for a future with potential full England recognition when the Left Defender made an incredible decision for an Oxford man – he went to Cambridge!?! Moving on to read for a degree in Theology, Tony spent a further three years in an area of study and life that was moving him away from his practical playing talents. He certainly responded to the academic demands of theology, but something was missing. From his early days on a very ordinary council estate, he needed to be near people and to help those in need. His approach had got to be how he intertwined his ecclesiastic message to the sectors of society that had confronted the hard and dark side of life. That was his goal. He was not naïve as he knew that this ministry may not be there from 'Day 1', but he had to travel down life's journey eventually to be in the midst of such hardship.

He became a curate soon after leaving Cambridge, having been ordained and taken on the mission at Edgware in north-west London. As effectively an assistant, he was learning a great deal about work in the community, and remember in 1979, this approach was not widespread with your local churchman who tended to concentrate their activity around the immediate church confines. After a further three years up in Stockport, he was entrenched in the demands of his work. Gone were the days of his meeting his other midweek passion of coaching hockey at Haberdashers' Aske School in Elstree. He would always follow the sport, but his dedication and undying commitment was now to the parish.

That parish would be Bacup, up there in the Rossendale Valley. A mill town in the 19th Century, its 20th Century form extended to producing a plethora of television's Coronation Street actors and actresses. This sense of affinity to the dramatic and the belief in the tight-knit community was served well by Tony's eccentric activities in his first week as the Vicar of Bacup.

As the Express Dairy milk float turned the corner of Nelson into Rosamund Street, out jumped two men to deliver the daily bottles of milk and other dairy sundries. Phil, the milkman, had been a regular to these backstreets for a decade or more, but who was his faithful milk-hand in those early weeks? Yes, it was Tony Porter! What better way to meet his new parishioners than early in the mornings on the milk round. He certainly knew his red, through silver to his gold top!!

The vicar became ensconced in this small town, a very similar place in the Pennine foothills that he had himself grown up in during the 1950s and 60s. Life was changing now with the old mills shutting down and a certain amount of net migration from Bacup to the bigger centres of Manchester and Leeds, and it was leaving behind and exposing needy communities as unemployment was biting into these towns. These issues were affecting families, and families were the mainstay of Tony's mission. His dedication to be actively involved and absorbing the pressures with those parishioners was widely appreciated and valued throughout the troubled decade of the 1980s.

If that was a challenge for him, the Church of England had news for him. "You ain't seen nothing yet!" or words to that effect!!

The 'Beirut of the North' where the crime figures stated below give a good indication alone, and these were taken from 2017 when crime had been halved over the period Tony was to act as the Vicar of Holy Trinity Platt, in one of Britain's most deprived areas.

Annual

Crime type	Total	Percentage
Anti-social behaviour	347	20%
Burglary	152	9%
Criminal Damage, Arson	181	10%
Theft	229	13%
Vehicle crime	121	7%
Public order	228	13%
Drugs	38	2%
Violence, sexual offences	441	25%

Tony Porter, Oxbridge graduate and hockey junior international had landed in Moss Side, Manchester!! This was to be his ministry for the next fifteen years up to 2006. Typically, Tony was to roll up his sleeves and take stock of his congregation and parish. The only way to achieve that was to be part of it, to live and reside and be visible to all amidst the wanton violence that the Greater Manchester Police was struggling to contain.

More poignantly, he and his wife, Lucille, were now also engaged in starting a young family with all the complications of schooling amidst a harsh environment of danger to the person.

Moss Side in 1991 was a multi-ethnic community of Asian, Caribbean and African migrants, interspersed with the Coronation Street community of Mancunians that had not escaped the two up, two down living in terraced slums that were erected in parallel street patterns from Victorian times.

Still, Tony Porter had the legal right as the Minister of the Church of England to knock on every door and he did as well. His message to the congregation at Holy Trinity was clear, that the Church family had to reflect the neighbourhood's cosmopolitan nature. Literally, parish members of colour just were not attending, even though they had followed the doctrines of Christianity, notably in their early lives from their native countries.

He had to appeal to them and to assure them there was a God for all the people, irrespective of their colour or ethnicity. Tony Porter was making that early impression amongst the locals and that mattered, but he soon realised that to achieve his mission, he had to work shoulder to shoulder alongside two big institutions that were central to the core of Moss Side life.

One was the Police, the Greater Manchester Constabulary. There had always been deep suspicion between the forces of law and order on the one hand and the community on the other. There were just too many misunderstandings, cultural differences, age barriers and frankly, blatant contempt on this south side of Manchester to provide a harmonious mix of people. It was multi-culturalism at work, where the Muslims lived and practised their lifestyle in one neighbourhood with the Caribbeans working their way of life in another. Add weapons and drugs as freely available and you had a recipe for weekly disasters and mayhem.

The Holy Trinity man stepped bravely into this void as an independent witness, literally. With so many teenage crimes making up the whole and with the environmental breakdown of the family, it was the police that were relieved to see Tony act as an independent witness for so many youngsters. Often it was a case of crimes being reported at all times of night to the vicar at his home. Then Tony contacted the police to report and mutually arrive at the scene of the most dreadful of crimes.

The Porter's family life would at best be reported as colourful, and at worst, as an intruded space for the ills and evils of the local community. Was that what the local Vicar was for? Slowly but surely he was seen as "one of us" and regarded as the Vicar who was always on the spot, not just at weddings and funerals, but at youth clubs, concerts and ethnic celebration events.

Still, the Vicar, rather pleasingly was missing something in his life, his passion for sport. Here in this tough environ, he was starting to realise that he and his parishioners were lacking open space and another element that can bring people together, the need for play and healthy competition. Equally he was seeing the role that sport could play in the lives of committed Christians. He looked around, and at the heart of Moss Side, was its connection to the outside world, its professional football club. Yet, like the area itself, Manchester City, was in the doldrums in the 1990s, believe it or not, stuck in the old Third Division.

It was time by the end of the decade not just to offer the much-needed improvement on the field, but to also view the Football Club as a whole, and in particular to investigate in detail its role and responsibilities within the Moss Side Community. Decay had become synonymous between Moss Side and "City". Huge turnover of managers had occurred with eight managers in just five years between 1993 and 1998. Then the Club employed former Everton favourite, Joe Royle, a very decent man who had a feel for that vital connection between the football club and its surrounding community.

Horizons were broadened and literally out of The Blue, the Club appointed The Rev Tony Porter as the Club Chaplain, a revolutionary move at the time. Yet there were many new features now as the Premiership was up and running, Euro competitions taking on vast TV audiences and revenues, and English fan bases were getting used to a larger number of overseas players and coaches with all their individual needs.

One major need was for spiritual and individual support. Tony Porter was to act in that background capacity as the independent minister who would deal with individual problems within the families of players, of overseas players' adaptations to their new base, and issues of faith. Still the former England hockey junior could never resist taking a peek at the training ground on a Friday, sharing his opinions on the preparations and indeed on the lunchtime menu. The typical banter of Alan Ball's time would continue under Joe Royle, with the players knowing that Tony had played top team sport. Mind you, he took a lot of stick about hockey being a girls' game from the Blue Shirts.

He also appeared regularly on the club's magazine and website, "Blue Moon", as one of the first chaplains to a professional club. There was the inevitable increase in 'street cred' for the Vicar as it took very little time for the huge fan base to recognise the bespectacled Vicar at every home game.

Inevitably, during his tenure under Joe Royle, Kevin Keegan and Stuart Pearce, there were fun times and hard times. Tony was now daily working with both extreme ends of society. His presence with the Moss Side residents really acted in strict contrast to the millionaire lifestyles of those that surrounded the players on the Maine Road stage. During his ecclesiastical ministries he was never to experience the situation in daily life of the disadvantaged poor existing so close to the affluence of the boardrooms at the Club.

He termed it servicing "the stinking rich with the stinking poor". This was serious stuff for him as his main raison d'être was to bring the two closer together in the band of faith. His ultimate friendship with the three outstanding managers of his time there ultimately helped as they struck up a close bond of mutual respect and understanding.

Manchester City Football Club sensibly gave the directive to the players that personal problems discussed with the Chaplain would stay with the Chaplain.

As manager Joe Royle noted, "He never pushed religion at them or to them. Most of all, they would divulge their problems to him, problems that sometimes it's not easy to discuss in a dressing room, or the Manager's office. He was and always will be of course, a messenger of God, but never pushed it to the young or senior players of our then troubled club. Around the corner at his Church in Platt Lane, he had his own problems to deal with, setting fire to the Church door, and theft, were all part of his everyday life! On reflection, I never heard him call one of these miscreants once, a raised eyebrow said everything.

I always knew that Bishop Tony is a man of many parts. He is a Community warrior, who mixes with all public services, Imams, Rabbis and thrills to a 5K run, he is a family man, who loves nothing more than a weekend with his children … grandchildren … and of course his wife, Lucille. He is a warrior for God in his pulpit and also a Referee of life who very seldom issues a yellow card, and never a red card! He never gives up on anyone."

There were fun times as well, inevitably with season ticket holders, the Gallagher brothers of Oasis and Ricky Hatton, the world champion boxer, witnessing the day the Manchester United team bus arrived at Maine Road for the Derby match. As the stars of their team descended from the bus, David Beckham, Ryan Giggs and Sir Alex Ferguson were greeted with a huge welcoming banner exclaiming,

"Welcome to Manchester!!"

As anyone in football knows, Old Trafford, the home of City's worldly rivals, lies within the neighbouring city of Salford!!

Tony Porter's time at Man City was in many ways stuck in a time warp just before the eventual move to the Etihad Stadium in Ashton in the east of the city in 2004. He did spend a couple of years there before his future destination in Nottinghamshire. However, it was never quite the same in terms of his connective work between an identifiable local atmosphere and its Maine Road football mecca. After all, he was not quite living on the job anymore.

Nevertheless, years into his new ministry as the Bishop of Sherwood, he still receives Christmas cards from Man City former players reminding Tony of his annual Christmas ceremonies and celebrations at the Club. Pertinent to his time in Moss Side, many of these cards and texts are addressed to him with the greeting, "To Dad". For many of those players at the time, that was exactly what he was, a father to the players and the community.

The Diocese of Southwell and Nottingham has over 300 churches or places of worship overseen by the Church of England. Under the auspices of the Archbishop of York, this was clearly a large and demanding area for Tony Porter to move into from the hothouse of Moss Side. Indeed, that description did reflect the full attendances at Holy Trinity during Tony's tenure. In simple terms, he had breathed fresh air into Holy Trinity and reinvigorated the tentacles that the church was able to reach.

While the same would be true to say about his decade in Notts, it would also be accurate to suggest that Tony Porter would return to his roots. That gnawing pang to follow and encourage sport was never far from him. Still an active sportsman himself and now with his four children themselves supporting young kids, sport was never far off the agenda, notably as he was officially now referred to as the Bishop of Sherwood. We all know that many blue moons ago, another benevolent sportsman used to roam the woods of Sherwood Forest, expert in the wiles of archery and sport!

For many years the Church had rather frowned upon and distanced itself from the professional world of active sport and its excesses. Likeminded Christians whose drive was often duplicated on the sports field never were organised as a movement or indeed even as a partner to sporting bodies. By 1984, Andrew Wingfield Digby had pioneered a charity called Christians in Sport as its first director.

The close nature of the connections that Tony Porter's life work between his faith, his living community and the role that sport could play, ignited the touch paper for prominent sportsmen and women to be far more proactive to promote their commitment to the cause. Cyrille Regis, Kris Akabusi and Bernhard Langar are all testimony to this strong bond and partnership between Christians and sport.

Tony was one of the pioneers of Christians in Sport and since his residence in Nottingham has created chaplaincies at Notts County, Mansfield Town and Nottingham Forest and, in his own words, always wanted to bring the message of the Gospels to young people on their terms and in such a way that they felt comfortable.

Happily, in 2015, with the supporting partners of Christians in Sport, Archbishop John Sentamu announced the new Church of England's Ambassador for Sport. Who was it? Yes, of course, it was Tony Porter. Straight away he stated that he wanted his sports ministry to be at the heart of parish and diocesan evangelism.

In his introductory speech at the Archbishop's Bishopthorpe Palace, in front of 36 delegates from all over the country, his motivation was made very clear in a language that every hockey player would understand. True to his beginnings, Bishop Tony insisted,

"We want sport to be at the heart of the parish, not on the wings, but in the heart of the midfield."

Chapter 9

Three Aussie Sheilas

Carol and Jean boarded the Britanis in the bright November Melbourne sunshine. It was late 1973 and still the days of the great ocean liners traversing the globe in a five-week passage from the docks in Victoria to the old country. Jumbo jets, the Boeing 747, were only introduced a year or two earlier, and were then only the domain of the rich and famous. That description had eluded the two young women as yet, but they still would have won awards for spirit and adventure to take on a two to three-month period of exile from Australia to the mother country.

Jean was simply revisiting her parents in the Welsh Valleys for an extended Christmas over her secondary school teaching in Melbourne whilst Carol was the crazy one. She sported a mini Afro hairstyle of auburn tinge along the lines of icon guitarist Jimi Hendrix. For her this was a trip of a lifetime and the chance to see a very different world from a very tightly-knit family in Victoria.

Whilst Jean was keen to pursue her teaching career, Carol had risen up the ranks of Victorian and Australian swimming and hockey, all before her 19th birthday. She had played for her State Under-18 team at the age of 14, and for the All-Australian U21 team by her 18th birthday. Her rampaging forward style had caught the eyes of the Aussie selectors and she was duly selected to play against the touring Canada and Scotland teams.

She had grown up as the daughter of an Anglo-Indian father and in a family where hockey was so important that they had moved house in Melbourne just to be located next to the hockey fields in her suburb. She recalls her early days in the game,

"We lived and breathed hockey, so I played juniors in my dad's team along with my brother only to be removed after the first three rounds because I was a girl and not welcome in the boys' camp. There were no junior teams for girls in those days and if you looked too good beating the boys, well that was not on!"

Dad, born in India, continued to coach at Dandernong Hockey Club right the way through to State level leaving an enormous footprint not only on his family's but on the State's elevation at national level in the sport.

Despite all this focus on hockey, social mates Jean and Carol had not been able to resist the urge to travel. Their deepest relatives were from the UK, in fact Carol was born there, so it was time to put their feet up for five weeks across Pacific and Atlantic Oceans on a cruise which would take in the Maoris of New Zealand, would perfect their hula-hula dancing in Tahiti, witness the extraordinary Panama Canal and finally test their nerves of averting the attention of uniformed Latin Romeos in Portugal.

They were young and ready for all the challenges of such a journey, and they needed to be as 'The Britanis' finally entered Southampton Water in mid-December. Oh, was it so dark, damp and cold, and true to form the British dockside labourers gave them a right royal welcome – a Go Slow!! Labour relations with management was producing a semi-strike. Finally, rid of the south coast sloth, they keenly wanted to take an early look at the Christmas London lights.

They had taken the train before Jean's uncle would pick them up from their London hostel. They drew the short straw here too, as the Lights never flickered in 1973 with blackouts, candles and imminent threats of the IRA bombing campaign. Undeterred, the two girls would enjoy their separate Christmas times, and with Jean introducing Carol to her friend's 17 year old daughter, Rowena, soon after the break, the three 'Aussie Sheilas' plotted their trip around the UK in Uncle Jim's red Cortina!

Their plan was to head up through southern England via Oxford and Cambridge, through Lincolnshire and Yorkshire to Scotland and back down through the west to visit relatives in St Helens in Lancashire before heading back to Wales. At first, the two Aussies were a bit apprehensive about young Rowena with the long blonde hair at just 17, but she had already left school and was still waiting for her first job. The journey would be a spark in the dark for her, and as Carol termed it, they were "three spirited hippies ready for anything!"

Jean, the downtrodden driver takes up the story,

"From Norfolk we were heading north to visit my uncle in Yorkshire when we passed a boy carrying hockey gear, and Carol insisted … loudly I remember … on us stopping to give him a lift. It was not our original intention to pick up hitchhikers. Still, we bundled him into the back seat with Ro and all our guitars and sleeping bags and blankets. Carol gave him the 'third degree', and discovered he was on his way to a hockey trial. So, of course, not knowing where we were, on a cold and misty, wet day, we set off for a place called

Scunthorpe.

That guy had no shame! He was running late, and with three healthy female onlookers, he just opened his bag taking off an England hockey blazer and stripped naked to put on his hockey gear! It was then that Carol had worked it out, he was an international player. I swerved into the Game Day car park, inundated with mud on bodywork and tyres, and he galloped free just two minutes before the start whistle!!"

Carol interjected, "He had changed our entire journey plans to fit his hockey trials in, but we watched him enthusiastically and he did play well, and no doubt the selectors could not help but notice him as every time he got the ball, the hippy cheer squad were hollering like banshees on the side-lines. We were Aussies and well behaved, well maybe not, but had a great time.

After the game, our hero came over and invited three dishevelled Levi-jeaned Sheilas into the team rooms. God, those guys were so posh that surrounded the players. We had never witnessed that type of hockey umpire, manager, coach or selector before. The food hardly touched the sides, we devoured it so quickly. The 'England boy' had a cheek, what a cheek! After his team won 3-0, he said in what I later learned was a Cockney accent, "ow 'bout kummin back for a few beers to celebrate?'

We didn't realise it then, but we were to head for a very different experience, a hundred miles north and in the hands of this clearly errant player, to sleep for two memorable nights on a student floor!!"

You know, what with the debacles with him and the showers and college food, it was 48 hours we would never forget, but it all seemed like another day at the office for him. I could never even remember his name. As for the three of us, he was another enigmatic ship that passed in the night of our youth and our wonderful trip which was to be rounded up by early February as "Cum on, Feel the Noize" by Slade hit the singles charts. We definitely felt his noise!"

* * * * *

The England Under 22 captain had just picked up his mail from the college pigeonhole.

"'bout bloody time, two day's warning for an England trial!"

He had been selected to play for The North v The East, a match between two of the top three divisions of English hockey. There was no British reserve or modesty with this lad who had given up everything London could offer to take up a University place to study in the north. Even though his mother was a staunch Northerner, he remained a true-blue Londoner.

For some time, he was pissed off with all the inevitable travel south to every representative game, so he had taken up the habit of hitchhiking to games, then claiming the generous expenses that the Hockey Association would offer to cover any costs. It really did make the difference on a student grant. This time he had to play in god-forsaken Lincolnshire on some steelworks ground.

He perused the map at breakfast that Sunday morning and with stick and bag in hand set off with outstretched thumb down the trusted A1. Everything went to plan as he was offloaded from one of those new juggernaut trucks by 12.15 just outside of Goole. Now the last part of the journey, no more than an hour to the Appleby-Frodingham Works for a 2.15 bully-off.

Nothing happened. By 1.15, shivering like an Eskimo, in his No. 1 uniform, he was starting to panic, as it was expected in those days for players to arrive at least 45 minutes prior to the start. Suddenly, a wreck of a Cortina passed him by, but shuddered to a halt fifty yards down the road. Three young women, piece of cake he thought, welcomed him into mobile Australia!

He issued the instruction quick,

"Can you take me to Scunthorpe and in time for the game?"

"We only picked you up because Carol is a hockey player", uttered the dark-haired driver.

Then Carol started to interrogate the fit young man as to hockey in England and how it compared to the Aussie version. The hitchhiker didn't get to believe all her stories of playing for Victoria and Australia, but only because she had a Jimi Hendrix hairstyle and anyway, he knew nothing about Aussie hockey at this stage.

"Hey love, do us a favour, put your foot down, pedal to the metal, and also, d'ya mind if I get into me gear in 'ere?"

The girls were taken aback. They were led to believe that all young Englishmen had manners, notably if they played a sport like hockey. This guy was different, almost rude, but there was an honesty about him that they enjoyed, apart from his jokes at the Aussies' expense.

Out the car he scrambled to join his teammates after a dressing down from the North's Manager. He was told he was not to play at centre-half, the playmaker of the team, but to be relegated to the wide left stopper position to mark England striker, Jimmy Neale, out of the game. He knew Jimmy from London days, a cheeky con-artist of a player who never tracked back if a wing defender should go forward with or without the ball.

That day was pivotal. The young left half scored two from open play in a 3-0 win. A small crowd whose noise level was boosted by three excitable Aussie Sheilas appreciated the young man's overlapping skills and as for the East's explosive England front three strikers, they were lambs to the slaughter with the North clean sheeting.

Carol, Jean and the blonde bombshell Rowena, invited into the post-match revelry, were the only females to be seen in the clubhouse.

The selectors, including an East stalwart, John Ivens, who was a right winger in his day, just could not believe a Cockney kid could wipe the floor defensively with their dashing East front three, and still have time to go up the other end and score two. He was too cocky for their liking, and fancy turning up to an England trial with three girlfriends. Better watch out for him in future.

The university lad somehow persuaded the girls back to his "patch" and in an all-male college smuggled them into his block to meet his roomie. He thought two guys and three game females in one student double room would be cosy enough. The next morning, he got up early to pilfer from the college kitchen a complete breakfast for five! Knocking on his door, with serviette and cutlery, he bellowed out, "Room service".

Still, could he negotiate a shower for the girls at the end of his corridor? Success, he thought, but one traitorous cleaner was to snitch on him to the Master of the College. It was in 1974, a sordid offence to have members of the opposite sex in your room.

The girls lasted another night before journeying on to Scotland. He had really enjoyed their company, their Aussie twang and in particular the one he called 'Hendrix'. Shame he never got to know her full name. As for his future in the College, England or no England, he was suspended after an interview with the stern, stuttering but amiable Master Tom.

The Master dressed him down for twenty minutes before committing the young man to a residential life out of college with the memorable line,

"You are unfit for communal living!"

* * * * *

The young perpetrator continued in the same vein, a thorn to all sides of management for another seven years in the up and down world of English hockey of the 1970s. He almost took on the role of shop steward, disagreeing with selections, training and match-play tactics of successive captains, coaches and managers, and there were enough of them. England's hockey management was like a revolving door in these times. So he quit.

The maturing rebel spent a decade on the road in and out of not so Great Britain in the sport and leisure business. His tentacles spread far and wide as he immersed himself in the expanding sports medicine business. The term 'sports science' became an evolutionary model as he pioneered notational analysis along with the science of vision and its offshoots in all the continents. In addition, he was quietly advising FIH coaching, equipment and competition committees on new and experimental ideas in these three vital areas of hockey.

By the mid-90s he was approached by a New Zealand businessman to act as a go-between to attract eight nations to compete in a new non-FIH Christmas 6-a-side tournament in Hong Kong, a direct parallel to the highly successful Rugby Sevens. He had consulted with a major synthetic turf company that had reached the stage to roll out a temporary carpet on a solid stadium base to offer a half-size hockey pitch. The teams would bring a squad of 10, with manager and coach and would mirror the nations of the rugby elite.

Brilliantly thought out as the stadium would be full each day as the pre-Christmas holidays would kick in with huge numbers of ex-pats from England, Ireland, New Zealand, India, Pakistan, Malaysia and South Africa would join with Hong Kong in a hockey sporting and financial bonanza. It was very much at the planning stage as one major hitch plagued the idea. Crowds, yes; pitch and stadium, yes; teams and quality hockey, yes; sponsors and Asian TV, yes; the hitch was the umpires who were not willing to jeopardise their FIH careers for an annual innovation in Hong Kong.

By now, our former England International had built up a network second to none in international circles, but particularly and deliberately outside of Europe, which he regarded as an inward-looking old boys' club for men and a 'ladies only' restriction for women. Then, at a coaching conference in Sydney where he delivered another radical clinic (How the Aussies loved a renegade Englishman) he met a man he could do business with. His name was Lance Forkgen, the Founder and Chief Executive of the Australian equipment firm, Just Hockey.

Often known as the Invisible Man, Lance portrayed many of the 'must haves' of a modern entrepreneur. He built Just Hockey up from the basement to be the biggest hockey outlet in the Southern Hemisphere. His start was a small office operating a gaggle of hockey associates responding to local and then State demands in Australia for a range of specialised hockey goods, sticks, balls, uniforms and goalkeeping gear.

His empire began in 1986, but soon he was to reach dream proportions by acquiring shops, mainly at the sprouting State Hockey Centres as part of the hockey experience. There was by the turn of the century no need for players to make special journeys downtown to select a new stick. It was all there at the Hockey Centre with Just Hockey exhibiting the complete range of imported sticks from Grays to Gryphon to TK. The Invisible Man would travel around the hockey world to secure deals cementing solid relationships with both manufacturers in Asia and with the final brand executives in Europe.

It was this direct connection between player and Just Hockey as "their company" that was the crucial factor as it exhibited at annual state carnivals across the country. For this first phase in its evolution, Just Hockey was just Aussie mate! Soon this was to change as Lance expanded into Just Hockey New Zealand and into the Pacific Islands as well. It was just a matter of time before the company would be a global brand in its own right.

He knew from the beginning that he was in it for the long haul and so did his colleagues across the world. From the outset, the Invisible Man would call equipment icons like Norman Hughes, then of Slazenger, and Neil Mallett of Grays International to seek out the latest trends and developments in Europe. Hockey, and particularly goalkeeping technology was to move on a pace after Ian Taylor had worn the high-density foam gear at the LA Games in 1984.

Lance witnessed Taylor fielding successfully 23 penalty corner Australian shots for the bronze medal and a GB victory. With the best strikers in the world, Craig Davies, Terry Walsh, Colin Batch and Ric Charlesworth, surely they could have picked off the pads for secondary goals. Trouble was, the rebounds came back at them with applied force as the foam did not only absorb but the return on the shots was clearing the Circle.

By Boxing Day, yes Boxing Day that year, Lance was on the phone at eight o'clock in the morning ordering 50 pairs of the new technology pad!! Typically, in Britain, Norman Hughes and Slazenger were only picking up individual custom orders! Australia in the form of Just Hockey had learned from their defeat, Britain meanwhile had just wallowed in the glory! Two years later, Aussie won the World Cup!

Lance in later years had ventured into new models of technology, highly specialised areas of the game to augment his catalogue. It was here where he developed a business relationship with our former England captain. Both men were prepared to risk, sometimes maybe too much, but the temperaments struck a common note as Just Hockey imported video materials and coaching aids from the UK which would be sold widespread across Australia.

The two of them would be seen together in off-hours as both could switch off automatically from business mode to the hockey international social scenes at World Cups and Champions Trophy events. Mind you, the Englishman never could match his Aussie mate well into the early hours at karaoke, where Lance would bring the house down with superb renditions of Engelbert Humperdinck crooner songs and his own favourites from the Country and Western world.

The familiar pattern of such meetings was broken when after a fabulous day at the Boxing Day Test at the MCG in 2005 v South Africa, Just Hockey were to invite the wayward visiting Pohm to an al fresco dinner date by the Yarra River that evening.

* * * * *

They were all there, friends and family, a table for 20 by the river with the flaring lamps as a startling backdrop. Lance at one end of the table beckoned a toast to the assembled throng to enjoy the banquet. Down the table, our former England man was positioned opposite a well refined almost shy couple, very well groomed but sociable, the middle-aged lady opened the conversation,

"Welcome to Melbourne, how did you come to know Lance, was it through Just Hockey?"

"Yeah, known him for twenty years now, quite a card, ain't he? We've had many a hockey social together. "Do the two of you play, any involvement in the sport?"

Stuart, the husband, replied in the negative but did indicate his wife had a thorough grounding in the sport. She took up the story.

"Well, I was a committed player once in my youth, played for Victoria State, but you know how it is, career, marriage, kids, but I do look back with great affection at my playing days all over Aussie. I even went to Pommieland once, but that was more travel and tourism."

"Did you see any hockey over there, when was it, back in the 70s?", inquired the visitor.

"Yeah, as a matter of fact we did, there were three of us touring the UK at the time and we did see just one game. Shouldn't say it in front of Stuart, but we picked up a hitchhiker who carried a hockey stick. God, he was mad, he kicked off all his gear in the car and it was true, he was about to play in an England trial."

"Blimey, I must have known him, what did he look like?"

"Strong bloke, long dark hair and sideburns, he played Left Half and I remember he was pissed off at that. He took us back after the game's reception to sleep on the floor at his college. Gee mate, he was out of his tree."

"What was his name?"

"Can't remember, but I know it began with the letter G, was it Graham, Gordon, Grant…"

"Maybe he had my name, Gavin? How does that grab you? Hendrix!"

Carol Daly, wife of Stuart, but born Carol Forkgen only sister of Just Hockey's Lance Forkgen had just fainted at the table. She had never known and nor had he!!

One for the cameras, Ash scores again for England.

His other sporting passion - Ice Hockey.

India Hockey League 'Player of the Tournament' with India national team coach Mahendra.

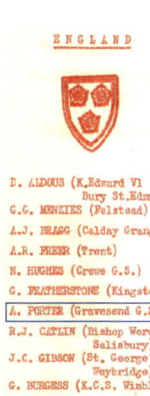

ENGLAND	IRELAND	SCOTLAND	WALES

ENGLAND	IRELAND	SCOTLAND	WALES
D. ALDOUS (K.Edward Vl Bury St.Edmunds)	A. PRESTON (Banbridge Acad.)	W. CHAPMAN (Fort Augustus Abbey School)	J. WILLIAMS (Christ's College Brecon)
G.C. MENZIES (Felstead)	P. ANDREWS (Methodist College)	G. LUMSDEN (Fort Augustus Abbey School)	R.J. YORKE (H.M.S. Conway)
A.J. BRAGG (Calday Grange)	A. MAIN (Kilkeel H.S.)	I. McLEAN (Strathallan School)	A. THOMAS (Cathays H.S.)
A.R. FREER (Trent)	R. PEACOCK (Bushmills G.S.)	G. McNAUGHTON (Fettes)	R.B. D.VIES (Liverpool College)
N. HUGHES (Crewe G.S.)	D. SHIELDS (R.B.A.I.)	D. GALBRAITH (Loretto)	K. PHILLIPS (Ruabon) Capt.
G. FEATHERSTONE (Kingston G.S.)	N. WALKER (Sandford Park)	A. STODDIE (Leith Academy)	R. FORMAN (Bridgend G.S.)
A. PORTER (Gravesend G.S.)	N. CATHCART (R.B.A.I.)	R. SIME (Grove Academy)	S. SPENCER (Bridgend G.S.)
R.J. CATLIN (Bishop Wordsworth's Salisbury)	S. WALKER (Sandford Park) Capt.	P. GRECO (Napier College) Capt.	J.C. REES (Liverpool College)
J.C. GIBSON (St. George's, Weybridge)	I. KIRK-SMITH (Methodist Coll.)	C. HEALY (Lawside Academy)	A. JEANS (Kingston G.S.)
G. BURGESS (K.C.S. Wimbledon)	A. HICKEY (Middleton College)	W. MILLER (Napier College)	P.N. JEANS (Kingston G.S.)
N.J.D. CLARIDGE (Bishop Stortford) Capt.	G. WATKINS (Avoca Kingston School)	D. PENNIE (Strathallan School)	S. BULLON (Kingston G.S.)
L.O. HUGHES (Haberdasher Asko's)	H. McCLEAN (Cork G.S.)	J. FINNIE (Geo. Watsons College)	A. BROWNING (Cathays H.S.)
J. HODGSON (St.Bede's G.S.)	M. McGONIGLE (Kilkeel H.S.)		S.EHAN (Cardiff H.S.)

UMPIRES : J.PIKE, ESQ.   R.G. BLOWER, ESQ.   H.J. ROTHWELL, ESQ.   P. ENGLISH, ESQ.
                                                                      E.S. WALL, ESQ.

THE BALLS USED IN THIS TOURNAMENT WERE KINDLY DONATED BY MESSRS. WILLIAM THOMLINSON LIMITED, GLASGOW.

Tony Porter – Champion Left Half.

Baz and the Bishop; "Tony was instrumental in my journey. He makes great things happen by connecting people. An extraordinary man in an ordinary world" – Marcellus Baz.

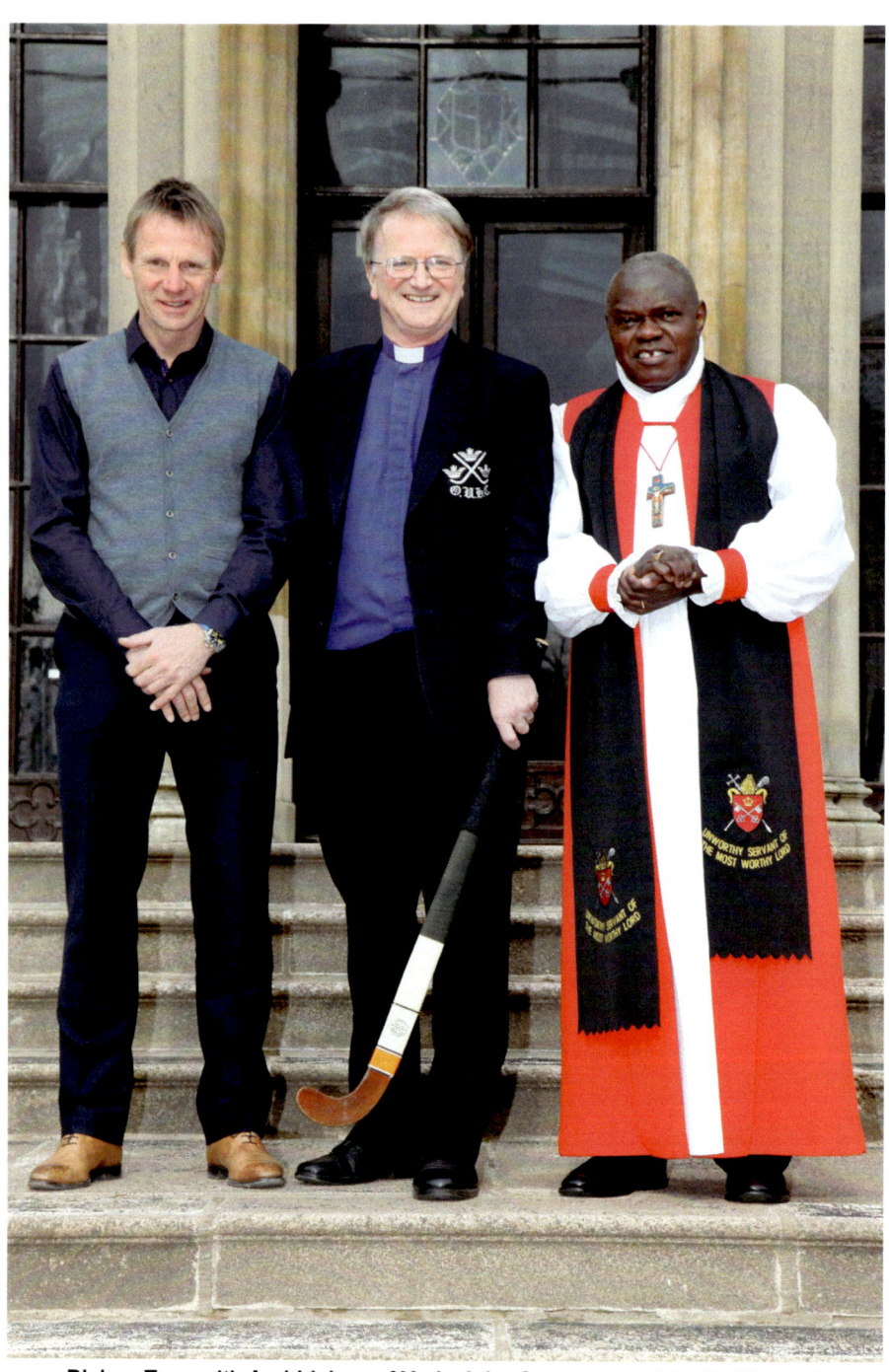

Bishop Tony with Archbishop of York, John Sentamu, and football legend Stuart Pearce.

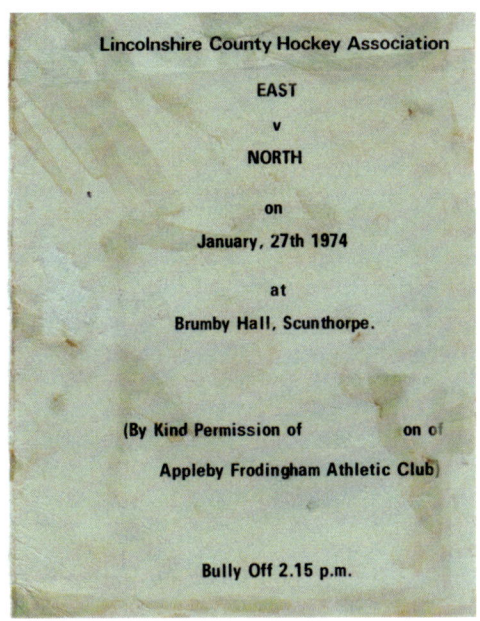

Lincolnshire County Hockey Association

EAST

v

NORTH

on

January, 27th 1974

at

Brumby Hall, Scunthorpe.

(By Kind Permission of   on of

Appleby Frodingham Athletic Club)

Bully Off 2.15 p.m.

Divisional games then acted as full England trials, even in Scunthorpe!

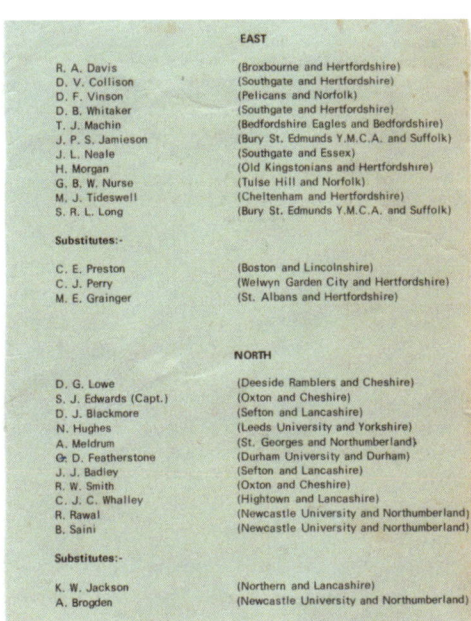

EAST

R. A. Davis	(Broxbourne and Hertfordshire)
D. V. Collison	(Southgate and Hertfordshire)
D. F. Vinson	(Pelicans and Norfolk)
D. B. Whitaker	(Southgate and Hertfordshire)
T. J. Machin	(Bedfordshire Eagles and Bedfordshire)
J. P. S. Jamieson	(Bury St. Edmunds Y.M.C.A. and Suffolk)
J. L. Neale	(Southgate and Essex)
H. Morgan	(Old Kingstonians and Hertfordshire)
G. B. W. Nurse	(Tulse Hill and Norfolk)
M. J. Tideswell	(Cheltenham and Hertfordshire)
S. R. L. Long	(Bury St. Edmunds Y.M.C.A. and Suffolk)

Substitutes:-

C. E. Preston	(Boston and Lincolnshire)
C. J. Perry	(Welwyn Garden City and Hertfordshire)
M. E. Grainger	(St. Albans and Hertfordshire)

NORTH

D. G. Lowe	(Deeside Ramblers and Cheshire)
S. J. Edwards (Capt.)	(Oxton and Cheshire)
D. J. Blackmore	(Sefton and Lancashire)
N. Hughes	(Leeds University and Yorkshire)
A. Meldrum	(St. Georges and Northumberland)
G. D. Featherstone	(Durham University and Durham)
J. J. Badley	(Sefton and Lancashire)
R. W. Smith	(Oxton and Cheshire)
C. J. C. Whalley	(Hightown and Lancashire)
R. Rawal	(Newcastle University and Northumberland)
B. Saini	(Newcastle University and Northumberland)

Substitutes:-

K. W. Jackson	(Northern and Lancashire)
A. Brogden	(Newcastle University and Northumberland)

13 internationals in the starting line-ups!

The most colourful shop in Australia.

With sticks aplenty at 'Just Hockey'!

Chapter 10

Highway to Hell

Lieutenant Colonel Brad Phillips began his descent of The Royal Air Force's new giant of the skies and banking to his left now had a clear view of what lay ahead, the RAF base and its runway at Oldenburg. The training flight had been a success, now all he had to do was ground the powerful single seat fighter plane.

At the far end of the tarmac was stationed Peter Charles and his awaiting fire crew, twelve lads in two vehicles that were always called to action stations when any exceptional flight was to undertake a landing. It was purely procedural.

Peter had now been stationed in Germany as part of his mandatory National Service for six months and rather begrudgingly had been allocated to the Fire Section of the RAF's contribution to NATO's defence on its northern flank against the Soviets. Surprisingly he was enjoying Saxony with a good set of mates and the additional bonus of picking up a new language.

The Hawker Hunter plane hit the runway a trifle fast with a resounding bump. Phillips assumed this was standard on a maiden voyage, but then the blistering pace of the craft rebounded and shook almost like a bouncing bomb. On the third contact, it descended into an uncontrollable skid with sparks flashing around him. The plane was reduced to a 'belly' landing. The undercarriage with all its landing gear, had been detached and was heading at over two hundred miles per hour directly in the line of Peter Charles and his crew parked only one hundred yards ahead.

They didn't stand a chance. The flying sheet of metal still with wheels intact cut through the two vehicles like a knife through butter. The casualties were appalling, six dead, three decapitations, the remainder set not to be conscious for weeks, permanently scarred.

Peter Charles was one of those, lying in a coma for over a month and a hospital ward for three. He had received multiple concussion and was never to hear again out of his left ear. The hospital staff did their very best for the eighteen year old, and at the end of his stay had pushed a Ministry of Defence form in front of him to sign for his exit release from the RAF and what he did not comprehend at the time, a pitiful pension of £2.65 pence per week.

How do you recover from that? There were no rehabilitation units, psychologists nor any aftercare in 1955. Peter returned to post-war Britain, still in some areas under food rations. For security reasons, he had to sign a declaration of no communication over what had happened at Oldenburg. The RAF had not allowed any visitors to his bedside during the whole sorry episode, except one important guy who insisted on paying tribute to the survivors, Lieutenant Colonel Brad Phillips, the American pilot.

It was on the last day of 'recovery', and along with an expression of admiration and sympathy, he let it be known that a full enquiry was underway with the American officials asking how 'fire trucks' could be located at the end of the runway with, can you believe it, an adjoining oil terminal only yards away. The only smile that Peter had mustered was when Brad told him that the RAF were for the high jump from their allied masters. The full force of the American Service personnel in occupied Europe was upon them.

Peter's demise, but not to his awareness, was to be a test case. Never again in military terms would emergency vehicles be positioned at the end of the landing area but enforced to travel parallel to distressed aircraft. Commercial air traffic would duly fall in line. Brad for some years became a pen pal with Peter knowing full well that the British establishment of the "you've never had it so good" years had covered up the biggest of cover-ups with Peter and his disfigured mates, the total embodiment of fall guys.

Peter Charles never moaned; there was no other way than to be welcomed back into Macmillan's Britain and keep a stiff upper lip and one functioning ear. His mum and dad still were living in a 'pre-fab', the temporary replacement dwellings set up for bombed out families down the East End of London. The good news for the family was they were to move up west to start afresh on the edge of South-West London on Britain's newly-built biggest council estate. There were two more pluses for Pete.

Firstly, he applied for and got after interview an apprenticeship with London's Metropolitan Water Board. He was to learn a trade, get a decent wage every Friday night and he could contribute to the upkeep of the family by giving half of his wages to his mum. That's how it was all done in those days, mum ran the house, dad had a river job down by Battersea Park. All seemed A OK, but as the years unfolded Peter could never hide his resentment for the British State and the instruments of its power or any form of the establishment.

His second reason for some future contentment was watching his kid brother grow up under the same roof. Thirteen years younger, "Fitz" was to experience his upbringing with Peter, sharing the second bedroom on the 10th floor of a "Point", Hindhead Point, a tower block on the Alton estate, one of the fifteen constructed at the end of the 1950s as part of Wandsworth's New World. Four rooms with a cubicle of a bathroom constituted a flat with a balcony with four flats to a floor served by one lift.

The Alton, Ashburton, Dover House and Danebury Estates were built around the small village of Roehampton, an enclave right on the edge of London, planned communities that would architecturally receive awards for their construction. They were to be a new way of living with the Danebury Avenue shopping arcade, the library and Roehampton Boys' Youth Club at the heart of a 12,000 population of 'new' people from the city. It was the planning dream of the French architect, Le Corbusier, an urban enclave surrounded by greenery. The Alton Estate boasted a functional modern whole with lungs to breathe on the fresh air away from the Victorian slums of Inner London.

If you looked on a map, Peter and 'Fitz' would spend their childhood by Wimbledon Common, a place Charles Dickens had once described as "wild and desolate". It had in previous centuries been a stage coach route between London and the South Coast, prone to constant attack by highwaymen, notably at a crossroads known right down to today as Tibbet's Corner. Prosecuted highwaymen were executed or gibbeted in the 18th Century where their remains were left suspended for all the passing public to record and behold! Even the local hostelries and 20th Century pubs were named after the area's repute, "The Highwayman" and "The Green Man" were thriving into the 21st Century.

Peter's generation, the last of the conscripted National Service, moved into the 1960s and were motivated to change the privileged world of entitled gentry, grouse shooting Prime Ministers and 'tip your cap' deference to your elders and betters. He himself was never going to do that. His temperament had become mild and mellow following his dice with death. It was just so sad to see him that withdrawn. Yet, by the mid-60s, he expressed himself in other ways, in music, in dress and in the way he moved across London.

Peter Charles was a 'Mod'. He had the looks, the sta-pressed trousers, the Ben Sherman check shirts, the Ivy League jackets and even a shiny pair of brogues. All with a slick styled crewcut hair style, a Parka jacket as overwear, and his pride and joy, his Lambretta Italian scooter. At last, he had found his identity, and on these London estates like the Alton, he could indulge with dozens of like-minded lads and girls. Friday nights at the Locarno, Saturday nights at the Castle Ballroom in Richmond was all he needed to blow his wages for the week. Ska rhythms and 'mod' bands like The Who, The Kinks and The Small Faces were the cornerstones of his existence, epitomised by the Mods' Anthem played out by Pete Townsend's "My Generation" single in 1965.

The Charles' boy knew he was a member of the promised land when his girlfriends shopped at Biba in Kensington, wore rebellious, revealing mini-skirts and would only watch their mum and dad's telly on a Friday evening at six o'clock to indulge in "Ready, Steady, Go". With a live audience, the presenter Cathy McGowan would introduce live acts and up and coming bands, like The Beatles and the Rolling Stones. Even England's football team had won the World Cup and here in London, the centre of his universe.

Yeah, that was his generation shoving it up his elders' backsides. All they had brought was war, misery and destruction to his way of thinking. His generation now had taken freedom by the horns and made London and Britain the world leaders in sport, music and fashion. Pete had got his mojo back, it had taken ten years, but he had done it his way and survived.

While he was tarting up his Lambretta with more and more mirrors and literally paying more attention to his scooter than his girlfriend, Jill Gibson, he used to watch his young brother, Fitz, playing football on 'the patch', a small area of council green land. They would arrive most evenings with one of those new plastic white balls and two-foot wooden stakes with which the council garden workers used to demarcate areas of 'no go' to the local kids. Fitz's big mates were Joe and Will Clark, Les, 'Paddy', the two brothers known as 'Mac' and 'Doc' and a little feisty kid they called Wally.

Their pick-up game was organised by 'Paddy' because he was the biggest kid with the Doc and Wally supplying the stakes as goalposts that they had nicked. 'Paddy' always split the two small teams into 'Sacred Hearts' and 'The Rest'. 1960s Britain was still very tribal. The Hearts were the Catholics that had gone to the local Sacred Hearts Primary, the rest of the group had 'studied' at the local authority schools like Elliott or Wandsworth Secondary Modern.

The group mirrored a generation of inherited tribalism of Mods versus Rockers, Stones v Beatles, Lambretta scooters v Triumph motorbikes, West v East, Chelsea v Tottenham. The elder generation had fought Nazi

Germany. What had Pete and Fitz's generation to fight, but themselves? Here was born the seeming need to have an opponent in daily life. The likes of Wally, Les and even young Fitz worshipped Peter and the culture he brought to the Estate.

They would play with Paddy and Les, trying to kick shit out of the younger real footballers, Fitz, Will and Joe, and to be kicked off 'the Patch' by the porter, who was council paid to look after the Point blocks as a caretaker. This usually happened as dark descended and Doc and Paddy would often argue the toss and occasionally chuck one of the stakes through the porter's ground floor window as altercations grew more and more numerous.

In summers, the gang would cross Roehampton Lane and go onto the edge of Putney Heath at the Punch Bowl, a bigger and better area to play and to meet up with some of their mates down Danebury. The boys now were getting older, most of them sixteen, and big and intimidating enough to get in the pubs with 'Paddy' who was already eighteen. Sometimes they would go there to "The Highwayman" after playing, others like Fitz and Will would return home.

One night they all believed that some distant observers at The Punchbowl were from the local boys' club or London Junior club "scouts" as they played. So 'Paddy' and Les left the game to find out who they really were. As the lads got within 20 yards of three middle-aged men, they scattered and took off in a panic. 'Paddy' gave chase for a short while with Les behind him, sneered,

"I hate those ...., you know what they were?"

Les did not respond. They returned to their game.

Paddy's adversaries that evening were now introduced into open society two years earlier. As a result of the Labour government's bill, the Sexual Offences Act of 1967, consenting adults of any gender were free to follow their instincts and sexual codes and preferences. Inevitably the liberal elite of politicians, artists and literary leaders were ecstatic at newly found freedoms, but such joy was nowhere near filtering down to such areas of working class estates where this gang of boys operated. They had been educated to ostracise homosexuals and their sub-culture. Indeed, they had received instructions for ten years in schools that it was illegal and immoral to engage in same sex relationships. Society had simply passed such attitudes down to them.

Added to the fact that paedophile men were out there interfering with young boys, was it really a surprise that young men were taken to vigilantism against the scourge, as they saw it, of young lads in their communities? Young practising homosexuals were forced to live a life in the shadows with clandestine meetings in public conveniences and after hours designated clubs in Central London. Tolerance for these activities was indeed a scarce commodity in Roehampton's Youth Club and working-class family communities for such a lifestyle.

None of this even bothered Fitz. He was only interested in sport and following the line of his brother as a 'Mod' approaching his seventeenth birthday. By now, Pete had left home, first working up in Central London, then a job in the Bundes Republic of Germany. He was now in his late 20s and still well turned out, wanted to branch out into adult life as a warehouseman in the dynamic growth of West Berlin.

Fitz missed him as a role model, a controlling influence on any wayward behaviour. Pete was well aware of the company his younger sibling was keeping. Most of them were just young kids going through this youth phase of their lives, but he also recognised two or three of them were hard core, nasty pieces of work who were exerting their views and violent ways on to easily-led foot soldiers.

Football matches at Chelsea and Millwall, rival gangs from Roehampton Mods clashing with the Worcester Park 'Greasers', and outings to Soho and Brighton were becoming regular fixtures for various members of the lads that Fitz was developing as best mates. By 1969, it was noticeable he was starting to get distracted from the one stabilising influence on his life, his education. Nevertheless, he went along with his parents' wishes that he must do well in his schooling.

This was Fitz's secret from the rest of his 'Point' mates. They would all leave school at fifteen, become carpenter's or butcher's assistants or act as "runners" in bit part offices in Battersea or Wandsworth. Fitz was different. He was passing exams, but never told his mates. He stayed on at school beyond the age of sixteen, unheard of on the estate. Remember in those days, only 7% of any year group would end up in further education. So, Fitz kept his secret to himself.

The Alton and Danebury Estates' adults rallied around Roehampton's pubs, The Earl Spencer, The Montague, and The King's Head where Fitz's dad had a part-time barman's job three nights a week. The kids were either making mischief at the Boys' Club, where the most popular activity was boxing or judo! The older ones gravitated to The Highwayman, their hangout, a modern pub with an "offie" on the side. They could take their old used bottles there and get the money back, a few pennies, but a useful way for parents to offset pocket money for their youngsters.

The usual mob were there on that Thursday evening, the 25th of September. They met straight after work, some of them hanging around kicking a ball about, others including Fitz and Will indulging in pints of lager inside the public bar. The barman was sharp as he knew which of them were eighteen, which were close, and the majority who still were nowhere near to drinking age. Fitz fell into the middle category as he was that very night celebrating his seventeenth birthday ahead of the weekend. So, for him, the weekend started on Thursday night, a warm up for the festivities with the family. Trouble was, he was still only seventeen, but he lied and got away with it as Will was nineteen and definitely with him at his table.

The boys were putting the pressure on outside. They knew it would be getting dark by just after 7.30 pm and they were all ready with the football and a number of those wooden stakes for goalposts.

"Come on Will, get a move on Fitz, we can play on the Patch tonight. Stuff that git of a porter, he's not interfering. If he gives us any bovver, we'll take care of him."

Both Will, at a 6.30 wake up for his apprentice job down Putney, nor Fitz were enthused. Fitz had school in the morning, a test of sorts at 9.00. The last thing he wanted was to get filthed up playing football and getting kicked around by Les and Co. For the first time, he just stood up to them and just reported he had a school commitment early in the morning.

"Stuff you Fitz, and you Will," was all he heard from the departing gang of the public bar, itching for a game.

The two of them remained behind supping their lagers. Anyone could see, even the barman, that these two were not the ones wearing turned-up Levis, braces and red Doc Martin boots. Their hair was longer, often termed as swede heads, their clothes a mile away from the 'hard Mods' with razor cut skinhead haircuts. The 'Mod' movement indeed had separated into two with Will and Fitz now much more interested in the more complex rhythms of psychedelic movement. Not for them radical stomping reggae, braces and boots.

They stayed at the pub longer than they realised. In a sense, it was a relief to get away from the group for once. Maybe, they too, were growing out of their lifestyle. Will walked back just before 8 pm to Dunhill with Fitz slipping over to Hindhead Point. They looked across and noted that "The Patch" was empty, none of the lads were there. Neither were the balls nor the stakes! Little did they know then what was to unfold in the next two hours.

Only later the following day, at first on the radio, then early in the evening papers and news on television was there the announcement that one of the most grievous crimes of the 1960s was to be broadcast to the shock and horror of all those on the Wandsworth estates, but also to the nation at large. It compared in its extremity to some of the heinous crimes of the Kray Twins and the Great Train Robbery.

Those alive at the time will remember it by its sheer viciousness where a pack of young teenagers set upon a passing man approaching Wimbledon Common via an underpass of the A3 leading out of Tibbet's Corner. There seemed to be no doubt that he had been a consenting male homosexual who had been on the heath by a lake which was a meeting place for gay men.

Evidently, he had parked his car on the Estate and was returning when he had merely stared at one of the boys. A chase ensued with four, if not more young teenagers involved. It was an horrific scene with multiple injuries inflicted on the unsuspecting victim. He had been beaten senseless with wooden stakes with diabolical blows to the head.

The guilty parties had left him for dead, a static figure laid across the concrete. There were no witnesses directly, but miraculously the victim had staggered up to a main road by the Putney Vale Cemetery Gates. Minutes later, an ambulance arrived and rushed the bleeding man to hospital. He died after a further two hours in the hospital bed from his injuries.

Fitz was dumbfounded, disorientated, he did no know what to do. Was it them or just some of them? After all, there were many other 'Mods' who had this hate thing going against those blokes on the heath. He went to see Will later that week, who felt the same, but all he could tell Fitz that the rumour on the Estate was that some, he did not know who, could have been involved. He also heard more hearsay that two of them had been arrested.

Neither Will nor Fitz were involved, but reporters and cameramen were all over the Estate trying to interview anyone, friends, youth club members and regulars at the pubs in Roehampton. Both their parents knew the crowd their sons were hanging around with, and disapproved, but everyone kept their heads down. They knew that none of Fitz's mates had ever been in trouble with the law, so it had to have been some other kids. As for their boys, they were wrapped up in bed that evening and Fitz had got through his test very well, thank you, that Friday morning.

After such tumultuous confusion, time flew past with Fitz and his parents even further shocked that the trial for a total of twelve teenagers was to be conducted at the Old Bailey, the most revered court of the British legal system. The kids on the Estate, Wandsworth Council, the architects, even town planners of this era all held their breath as sentencing was to be held in January, the first month of a new decade.

The press had stirred the whole trial up to fever pitch as they claimed it was not only the boys that were on trial, but much broader issues in society as well. If America was to have its soul-searching through Vietnam, what in turn was the future for the other great bastion of fair play and culture, Britain, experiencing when its youth could deliver such "barbarism"?

All stood at the Old Bailey as four defendants were to hear the verdict for the offence of murder, whilst the other eight faced the charge of conspiracy to commit actual bodily harm with possession of offensive weapons, namely pieces of wood.

One of the accused was handed out a life sentence of 30 years, three boys under eighteen were ordered to be detained during their Majesty's pleasure, and the remaining eight sent to borstal.

Summing up, the judge in passing sentence said,

"I have to consider not only the accused and their unhappy families. If law and order is to be maintained either in schools or in particular neighbourhoods, the longer one holds back from deterrent action the more difficult it becomes to restore a civilised state of affairs. Twelve youths went to a popular open space for the purpose of finding someone to beat up with the result an innocent man lost his life. In order to protect the public, I must pass sentences of custody and hope such action will make the public open spaces round London a safer place for all to use."

All twelve guilty boys had reached a crossroads so early in their lives, and all of them with intent took their choices and options that September night. The result was clear to see, they had to front up and take responsibility for their actions.

Fitz faced the same choices that evening. He could or might have ended up on that desolate common, but he didn't. He had kept his secret. He did have a school commitment that following day.

He was to play hockey, of all sports, for his school team.

He dreamt that one day he would play for England. Did he? I don't know if I should tell you this. As it happens…!!

Chapter 11

Dutch Courage

Kingston G.S, Millfield, Whitgift or Repton School, take your pick, but what about Oulder Hill Community School in Rochdale?

Before you ask, you're right, as they don't even play hockey there. No fees, no double Astroturfs, no to much in life, but today one of their favoured sons has to ward off autograph hunters in one of Europe's greatest cities.

Simon Egerton, Edgy to his mates, was rejected by the holies of England Hockey to take up residence in Rotterdam and shoot literally, to stardom in the Dutch Hofdklasse and Euro Hockey League. Yes, that was his triumph, but his struggle represents the ultimate example to young players never to lose faith and persevere, whatever is thrown against them.

He grew up in the former mill town, one of three boys to an internationally playing Dad. Mike was a razor-sharp centre striker with a keen eye in the circle for scoring goals, a quality that he passed on to both his sons, David and young Simon.

The bloodlines led straight to the hockey goal. Dad distinguished himself at England U21 level, then had the audacity to gain employment in Scotland. He never was scouted thereafter let alone contacted by the England hierarchy, so, positively he took up nationality as a true Scot. Well he was born in Wick!

Little did their father know then, that his youngest son was to experience the English disease himself. Both David and Simon through their Manchester club, Bowdon, achieved junior level success with England by 2005.

Then, could Simon, like all young aspirants, make the transition to senior hockey? His Bowdon club had pushed ambitiously into the top flight, the Premier League. Spearheaded by Raj Toor and Manager Bill Ball, the club believed in and backed their group of young players. They became a permanent fixture in the Prem, but still no recognition for the free-scoring midfielder Simon Egerton.

Inevitably a young player must glance across at the fortunes of the National team, and in 2009, England won the European Cup for the first ever time. With the London Olympics three years off, it was great timing for the Coach and his group of solid players. They included two superstars, Ashley Jackson (read "England's No 7") and the evergreen Barry Middleton.

Simon could see they were both midfield men, and with the coach staying loyal to his 2009 group, there was a 'no entry' sign. Could and should he move up as a striker, perfect his drag-flicking and take up a new role at Beeston? He did, and in just one season was the leading goal-scorer in the Premiership as he was in the Australian National League years earlier. Surely, his goals would be noticed, but before the London Games, the Coaching staff's answer was, "OK, but the League's level was too low!!"

All this suggests by the age of 27, Simon Egerton was not a Yes Man. His adaptability, fitness and goal-scoring abilities were beyond question. No Olympics in Beijing, no World or European Cups, and tragically No London in 2012.

The last chance saloon was the new 2013 squad of 28 players, fully contracted to Rio on a four year yield, but after a disastrous Champions Trophy where England, with Simon, bombed in Melbourne, that was it for the 28 year old.

He was aged-trapped! New Coach Crutchley, said adios to the late 20s Brigade, and pushed a new set of Loughborough trained youngsters. Young coach, young team! And guaranteed through to Rio. A free ride.

The Eng-e-land was now, for Simon, a No Man's Land. He had been well and truly buried. Yet, there was plenty of fight left in him yet. Realising his fledgling England career was over, could he resurrect it in a new land? He wanted to stay within touching distance of his own family, not just parentally, but with the many hockey friends he had gained in English hockey.

Even if the English would not open their eyes, there was one country at the head of the queue for his services: – a little 'ole hockey nation called The Netherlands. Risk is part of their national story, and in hockey, they had transformed ten years earlier a brilliant young Scot, rejected by Great Britain, into a full Dutch international. Lawrence Docherty had been there!

Bram Lomans and H.G.C. in The Hague had Simon's card marked: – "you're here to score goals," and guess what, he responded in the toughest league in the world as its top scorer! The word spread quickly. Simon had shown Dutch Courage to risk everything, now it was payback time, and in 2014 he was to hit the jackpot.

It is easy to suggest here and give the impression that Simon was self-sufficient, but he, as a single bloke, would be the first to recognise the support he received from his mother Audrey, who actually started the Women's section at Bowdon HC and that assistance from his Dad and the family of players at Bowdon.

Family, it seems to have taken on so many meanings these days, but if defined, it is a support system. At this stage, he needed people to believe in his talents and encourage them to the full. Holland became Simon's family. The country for over a century had fallen in love with hockey and what it brought to these 'Neverlands'.

In every club, the elders passed on to the youngsters great sporting values and standards, both on and off the pitch. They were forever young with a true cross-section of ages across what was as much a social as a hockey club.

In short, Simon was to land on his feet where the Club was the ultimate family. His choice and it was a choice, was to be Rotterdam HC. Fifteen years earlier, the Club had sold up its original venue to the new Amsterdam – Paris fast rail link. The deal yielded the Hockey Club a fortune to move to new flat lands! Within two to three years, there were 9, yes nine, Astroturf fields on their one site, including three water-filled.

The dynamic Chairman handled all these affairs and set up an ambitious programme to take the Club to the top. Jan Hagendijk steered the site as a venue for the newly established Euro Hockey League, drew top foreign internationals from all five continents to Rotterdam, and really set new targets and horizons, even by Dutch standards. World Cups came to Rotterdam with the club harnessing a total of beyond 2000 members.

For Simon, despite his successful travels through Germany and Australia, this was a new ball game. With a marvellous year behind him at HGC, Rotterdam posed new challenges.

Contracted for the next three years, he had something to live up to, as previous foreign players included the likes of Mark Knowles the Aussie legend, Simon Child of New Zealand, and the Pakistan Corner ace Sohail Abbas. These exponents were paid well with a total team annual budget of €800,000, a phenomenal amount for just the wages of players and coaches. Yet, with that injection of finance went expectation. The Dutch members would demand quality of performance when a third of the squad were from overseas destinations. Still, the rewards for the young Englishman were great.

He always contended that he had moved to Holland to better himself as a hockey pro. Now, what were the trappings of being a pro in the Dutch system of "Top Hockey"?

Simon faced a world surrounded by professionals from the first signing of his contract through to the various personnel that were to shape his hockey for the next three years, that is three years if he was to be successful for the club. Make no mistake, the Manager, Coaches, physical trainer, physiotherapist and videographer were all in place with one end in mind; that of gaining a place in the Hofdklasse Top 4 and the chance to play in the Euro Hockey League.

This European dimension was not just a vehicle of status. All EHL games and notably the opportunity to host later rounds were a big money-spinner as the crowds would roll in at will. The Netherlands' hockey bandwagon was at the heart of Europe, and the top clubs in Holland like Bloemendaal, Amsterdam, Den Bosch, Kampong and Rotterdam expected success.

To ensure this could occur annually, training was set at three to four major sessions mid-week to prepare for the weekend. Squads of 22 contracted players would compete with each other for the coveted match play at weekends. The training was with ball in selective parts of the field in small areas where short play was encouraged, always in contested situations.

Every three weeks there were fitness tests for the players to sustain their levels throughout the season, invariably with body fat and interval training tests and times. The coaches came into their own in specific video programmes for the players both in a collective environment and through individual outlets.

With the overseas players, at Rotterdam, it was not a prerequisite that they coach down the club, but Simon was keen to join an army of volunteers, in heading up the Boys Under 18 group.

"I thoroughly enjoyed this aspect of my time here, and the spectator numbers for weekend junior games exceeded any games in the Adult English Premiership!"

Parents, friends, relatives flocked to the matches in support of their kids as they progressed through the club. The ultimate for them during the year would be an invitation to train with the Seniors, surely an indication of things to come?! It had been a long road at these expensive clubs since starting at the age of six to get to this stage, so with affiliation fees, tours, tournaments and equipment, hockey at Rotterdam remained very much in the middle-upper income brackets.

Critics of these élite clubs may have a case when it comes to the point that they are restricted to a narrow band of society. True, but let it be stressed here that these same people put back their hard earned money back into the clubs. In my parlance, "they put their money where their mouth is", and that cannot be said for the richer elements in the UK, Germany, Ireland or today's Spain.

Rotterdam is a classic example of the club's parts making up an integrated whole. The Euros, the sponsor's finance, the facilities, the junior development, the staff and the teams all were interdependent.

It is a business, but here's the rub. Simon found an incredible social community here, that were willing to assist his adaptation to and enjoyment of a new country. Certain Dutch traditions have stayed with him as unforgettable memories of hockey in Holland. These include the crates of beer in the changing rooms after the most intense of matches. Following that, the weekend entertainment continues with the "Thé Dansants". The best way of describing the latter is to imagine a barn dance with thumping music and a great deal of liquid refreshment!

The Thé can, on Sundays, go well on into the night, and represents the highlight of the social week for many, many hockey players, whatever their standard.

The match play of the Hofdklasse is put out weekly on terrestrial TV by commentator Jacques Brinkmann, and there is a Match of the Day Highlights programme as well as two Live Games broadcast at weekends.

Suddenly, Simon Egerton was in a whirl of activity, but with an apartment and a car as part of his deal, he was sailing on into the zone with security at his back. In his first two seasons, it was bonanza time as Rotterdam pushed into the top four with his name regularly on the team sheet. England was just a fog now in the mists of time.

He would argue that the foreign legion of Rotterdam including Aussies, Spanish, New Zealanders and British were tipping the balance for the club. They brought diversity of skill sets, wide match play experience, set play specialists, and made a great impact and influence on the young players at the club. Committed overseas players could do this especially if they were more of a medium-term package of consistency: e.g. three-year contracts.

Yet there were always the one-year wonders or those that maybe did not adapt or even worse, did not perform. Simon palpably was not one of these, but he did walk into a form of hockey storm in recent months and not of his own doing!

After the club penalty corner specialist was recalled to his own country, Simon was elevated by the coach to take the Penalty Corner duties, but this was ahead of a native-born Dutch National player and a famous, well-connected one at that!

The National Team Coach intervened to show his frustration at yet another foreign exponent replacing Dutch nationals at the vital set piece in the game. To Max Caldas, the long line of Kruise: Litjens: Bovelander: Taekema was a given for the method of the Dutch stamp on the game. Now the foreigners, and note Max is an Argentinian, were denying that National Right to be at the sharp end of the game, the Drag flick at Penalty Corners!

Remember, it was Simon's Rotterdam Head Coach that had made the decision based on what was right for his club, and the Engels man was scoring goals! The confusion was exacerbated by the Rotterdam's Coach other position in hockey: he was the KNHB's Assistant Coach to the Women's National Team! As Johan Cruyff used to say, "everyone in Holland has an opinion on sports."

The ongoing incident has, however, touched on a Dutch nerve. There are no limits on overseas players, and notably amongst the country's elders there is growing concern that young Dutch talent is being temporarily halted in its development, particularly in men's hockey, at vital stages. Simply put, young potential Dutch U21 players are not starting as core team members within club hockey's hofdklasse.

Memories are long here. The hurtful 1-6 Final defeat in the home World Cup in 2014, and the lack of real success in Rio has prompted many to assert that external Dutch hockey is suffering as a result of the invading hordes! No one has really noticed much difference, especially when the Euro Hockey League, this year in 2018, has yielded three of the four finalists from the Netherlands – Bloemendaal, Kampong and Simon's club, Rotterdam.

Edgy now is approaching his zenith with his team across the North Sea, though he retains that air of a modest Englishman abroad.

"The squad expect me as a striker to be on the very end of everything, tip-ins, rebounds, defensive errors. Then of course, not only to win Penalty Corners, but to score from them as well!"

He puts the success of the club down to averting and overdependence on two or three players but stressing the ability of its team members in all parts of the field. He remains the top scorer, but at the age of approaching 33, time no longer is on his side. His four-year adventure hangs in the balance as the team approaches the Euro Finals with its new experimental points for goals. In one qualifying game the scoreboard read "Rotterdam 20 Three Rock Rovers 10"!! Three points for a field goal, one for a Penalty Corner!!

What did Rotterdam's No. 9 think?

"Like all the Umpires and Coaches, the team's players were not just negative in getting their heads around it, they wondered who let the nutters out of the asylum!"

He did understand the motive behind it but pointed out that the average number of goals per match in the Hofdklasse was six, a healthy return. Surely that meant hockey was in good shape.

Without doubt, it has been Simon Egerton who has positively contributed to that fact over the past four years with his incisive approach to striker play. He has taken all the opportunities laid open for him in his adopted hockey nation. It was Holland's gain and England's loss. Thank you, Oulder Hill School, Rochdale!! Dank U well!

He found freedom on the field of play with coaches and spectators demanding quality from him in the most competitive of environments. They backed him with his skill set to perform and achieve. He did!!

We left a dark 1890 restaurant outside the world-famous Wagener Stadium in Amsterdam that spring afternoon. Edgy turned to Gav, "Something to add! There's one thing I still never have got used to..."

"Yeah, what's that?"

"Everywhere I go, the boys and girls stop me in the street and want my autograph."

Chapter 12

Homerton Home

As the entourage of England Hockey's Chief Executive Officer swooped through the car park gates of the Olympic Park, they took up their allocated position by the 2012 stadium. They walked with that confident air of officials at this latest of summer tournaments, the sense that this was their throne, their reward for a job well done. It was to their minds, the current home of English Hockey and nothing was going to remove them from the gravy train of Committee England.

Why should they worry? The day-trippers were there with bums on seats paying over £30 per head per day even though the 2012 Games were a distant memory and the National teams were at best struggling to stay at the top table of international hockey.

Had they bothered, a glance across the bright blue turf and down from the surrounding stands in the shadow of the London stadium was the border between the sport of hockey and the Borough of Hackney. Across that divide was what made Hackney famous, the Marshes. Dozens and dozens of football pitches were underlaid with an incredible drainage system of WW2 rubble from the incessant incendiaries of the German Luftwaffe.

For the entirety of the 20th Century, right down to today, the kids and adults of the Borough along with a multitude of teams from adjoining Newham, Islington and Tower Hamlets would trudge down to the Marshes to play their weekend football. On Sunday mornings at its peak, the Hackney and Leyton Association would be hosting over 80 teams at this mecca of the East End. All that grass, but hockey was not for Hackney and Hackney definitely not for hockey.

From the glittering stadium for Olympians, just take the Homerton Road, a mile at the most into the centre of the Borough and all you will find today is old terraced housing interspersed with estates slung up after the war. There is hardly a spare blade of grass, so where there were pre-war factories, now we can only see housing estates from different eras of construction.

The most notorious of which is the Kingsmead blocks of flats, cheap units that have assimilated over the years some of the poorest communities of Britain. Post war penniless EastEnders have gradually given way to waves of migrant populations from the Caribbean, Africa and the East Indies. As this process of cheap council rents allied to often transient inhabitants who may not have had an identity with such a neighbourhood, crime and slum conditions prevailed. The spiral to despair with violence, drug dependency, suicide, gang warfare and the breakdown of family a common daily reality, it comes as no surprise that Hackney boasted the lowest level of educational attainment and the highest level of crime of any London borough.

Throughout the 60s right through to the turn of the 21st Century, the Borough was caught in a never-ending rut of its inability to attract both sufficient government investment and commercially upward activities which would stimulate local growth and stability. The Hackney Educational Authority for decades ran a different regime to other London boroughs, an overseer which was often politically rather than educationally motivated. Old decaying buildings prevailed with schools' budgets often directed into peripheral projects rather than improving the basic fabric of curriculum, learning and social cohesion.

More kids left school proportionally at the age of 16 with few qualifications. Tertiary education was just a dream. In secondary education, there was a huge turnover of staff as the teaching vocation was to be more of a daily war in attempting to keep control in the classroom and in trying to keep crime away from the gates of the school. Even today if an interested reader wished to explore a neighbouring schools' website of Danesford School in Bethnal Green, they would note the upfront boast of prominent alumni with the Kray Twins as gangsters to the forefront!

It spoke volumes that the Borough of Hackney's Upton and Brooke House schools produced the famous playwright Arnold Wesker, and the celebrity 'Apprentice' Alan Sugar, and a host of professional boxers and footballers. These were all self-made men that delved deep into both their natural talents and more to the point, their drive to push on upwards and out of Hackney.

The trouble was, throughout these decades, the schools and the Community were failing whichever yardstick was considered. Only teachers with a deep conviction and dedication, and administrators on a selfless social mission could survive. So what chance hockey, a game certainly up to the 1970s that was associated with the Toffs and educated schoolgirls? The Hockey Association (Men) and the All England Hockey Association (women) had not even got their act together as one, with a state of mutual disregard existing between them. Hockey was a non-starter.

Then came along a voice in the wilderness, a pied piper called Martin Foxall. He was one of their own. Growing up in neighbouring Wanstead, Martin had left school with one 'O' level, but he had inherited a degree of family success through his granddad who had ventured into property in Silvertown and a father who had been on West Ham's books. 'The Fox' on leaving school at 16, had gained a job in the City as an accounts clerk which moved him on and bounced him around throughout the 1960s. He would rise early to get back home after ten in the evening. Determined to end the decade on at least £10 a week, his rejection of convention and set hours propelled him in 1970 to £1,000 per year, the startling sum of £20 a week.

He always wanted to continue playing sport in his spare time, notably as he had picked up quite a bit at Loughton School in football and hockey. If he chose one, it had to be hockey, but their clubs were situated further out in the 'sticks' cosily located in the posher suburbs of Ilford and Loughton and Woodford. Would he fit in, could he fit in?

Most of the team members were middle-class, much older and wiser than the young, impatient Foxall. To his chagrin, there were no real leagues, just 'friendlies' and precious little attempt to improve the technical advancement of the players. The furthest you got in that regard was a word in your ear over a glass of ale in the clubhouse bar. The Fox appreciated all that tat, but he was a competitor and he wanted an outlet for this aspect of his personality.

He did, however, note one element of his experience in British club hockey and that was the way these people carried themselves. Win or lose, there was always a modesty and a priority to comport yourself appropriately. He learned to be modest in victory and to take defeat as a challenge for the future.

However, as a principled individual, he felt he had to learn more about the game. So he enrolled on one of the forefathers of English coaching methods, a John Cadman coaching course aimed at school and club development.

"The only real reason I wanted to coach, was to avoid getting dumped upon every game as a player!", so there was clearly a practical motive as well.

As the 70s decade unfolded, he was getting more and more frustrated with his day job in the offices and therefore began to explore the possibilities of part-time coaching alongside fellow luminaries like Harry Stone. He acquired, despite not having any formal teaching qualifications such jobs with part-time attachments like Wadham Lodge. Little did he know then that this step into the darkness was to launch him into a four-decade career.

1980's Hackney was a dark place. A whole sector of schools was either failing, closing, or integrating under a new name. At this stage, this was the foremost method of change by the Hackney Educational Department. The maxim was to rebrand the school with a new name. Thus, the local pair of schools Upton and Brook House were to amalgamate, if only comically to stop the "Ice Cream War" between two rival Italian ice cream vans which used to supply the schools in summer term. They would vie for the kids' custom outside the gates at lunch times.

All seemed innocent enough, but rivalry turned to street violence and vandalism as the ice creams were subjected to sabotage, robbery and Mafia-inspired in-fighting to control their patches of operation. Only in Hackney!!

Thus, Upton and Brooke House became Homerton House School. Initially there was opposition as it meant a great deal of disruption as again rival factions were housed under one roof. Soon Martin Foxall was to bring his brand of discipline, street discipline to the 'new' school both in physical education and in the 'clubs' he offered four nights a week after school.

His direct no nonsense approach attracted the kids to a ropey old sloping playground, not even an eighth of the size of a full pitch. The school did not like the idea at first of hockey as in this part of the world, hockey sticks would be used as weapons. 'The Fox' used his ingenuity and approached a sports outlet in Walthamstow called Sedgwicks. Out of his own pocket he bought 300 ramshackle sticks with no labels for 35 pence each!! He kept them all in the back of his van.

He laboured hard for several years concentrating on skills, attacking skills that from a young age he had admired from the Indians and Pakistanis. Strict behaviour codes were enforced and any lack of discipline from his 11 to 16 year old boys he clamped down hard upon. Soon he was fielding teams that could occasionally play at Wadham Lodge's pristine grass fields or on a newly built water-based surface, with no water provided, at Mabley Green next to the Matchbox factory!

Suddenly a group of lads were to reject the Marshes at the weekends and put all their energies into hockey. Names like Dominic Camillieri, Mark Donnelly, Chris Gladman, the imperious Steve Ashton and perhaps the most well-known to followers of hockey in England, Nicky Thompson. Foxall was not just a coach and trainer to these Hackney lads, he was a real substitute father. He guided them away from trouble, instilled personal and collective discipline and soon they were all to play for England's junior teams.

Playground hockey was to win them over again. Meagre beginnings supplanted with dedicated teacher hours beyond the classroom had won the day. As Martin was to discover, it was a day to day existence. Even in Nick's case, the evening before an England U18 trial, he had raided a nearby shop with a group of mates seeking videotapes by the score. They inevitably, loaded, made a run for it with Nicky escaping the cops by clinging to the underbelly of a car as searchlights and torches patrolled the local car park.

Gang warfare continued, and it was not unusual at Homerton House to hear the clicking noise of police helicopters land to arrest schoolboy suspects. Again, in Nicky Thompson's case, one England U21 training weekend at Lilleshall was interrupted by the police enquiring if there was a Mister Thompson was on the field! He was to help the London Met with their enquiries!!

Yet the firm hand of Martin Foxall was always a deterrent. He was never past clipping the lads when they needed and deserved it, but this was always achievable as he spoke their language, on their terms, making a diverse bunch of Hackney boys responsible for their actions. Still, by the mid-80s he had the players but not the fixtures. No state schools in Hackney had boys' hockey; yes, he got the boys attached at club level to Ilford and the Old Loughtonians, but he needed school matches to match the ambitions of Ashton, Gladys and Tommo. He could not let them return to the likes of Clapton Rangers and their like on the windswept Marshes weekends.

The Fox befriended David (Vinnie) Vinson, a wood merchant from Kings Lynn who had risen from the East to national coaching prominence. Vinnie was an ideas man who religiously retained his influence within the East of England. Like so often, the two of them were made for each other, a hockey double act. Vinnie needed the element that Hackney boys would bring to his coaching stage, which had so far been dominated by Cambridge chaps and the independent schools of Bedford, Ipswich and Essex. Martin, in turn, simply wanted David's network, his sphere of influence.

Soon mighty St George's Weybridge, Whitgift and the almighty Felsted were on the Homerton House fixture list. They, of course, would never come down the East End. One match in the school's calendar was at Felsted, where Martin took his Under 16 team to the backwaters of Essex. On meeting a distinguished 'shirt, collar and tie' in the clubhouse after the game, he was asked,

"How did the game go, ole boy?"

"4-0", replied Martin,

"Oh, I am sorry, better luck next time, ole sport,"

"No", interjected the Fox, "4-0 to Homerton House!"

"Where the dickens is that?", the former colonel asked,

"Acknee, a comprehensive school in the East End", he replied,

"What is the world coming to?" concluded the man in the Barbour jacket.

Tommo and the gang had done the gaffer proud! Even the highly respected and affable Nick Irvine, the TV hockey guru, and the manager of the Under 14 England Independent Schools team waived the rules and invited Homerton House Boys to tour with the privileged set. For the likes of Camilleri and Thompson, it was a case of play hockey and see the world outside of their Homerton Home. They both would go onto play for England, Tommo all the way as England and Great Britain's Centre Forward between 1991 and the turn of the millennium.

Tommo, having chosen hockey as a playground option over cross-country was to be a role model for succeeding groups of players from Homerton. Like many of his peers, he was the product of such estates as the Kingsmead, a lad alongside six brothers and sisters from two independent fathers.

"I am blessed, Gav, I owe it all to Martin. He really took me off the streets and gave me and scores of others real values for life. Just look at the blokes you know he's coached, he even had the sadly departed Ugo Ehiogu playing for the school hockey team and he became an England footballer and inspirational youth coach at Tottenham Hotspurs. He was a Hackney boy!"

The old borough was changing and evolving into the 21st Century. Always diverse, but either side of the millennium new waves of migration were moving in alongside the original Afro-Caribbean influx of earlier times. Any photographs, see photo page, reflect these changes with huge numbers of Bangladeshi people now playing a prominent role in Hackney life.

Whereas it was difficult to prize white and black lads away from the Marshes and football, Martin Foxall was to continue his hockey missionary work in the Homerton environment with predominantly Asian-based teams. For Hackney's educational services and Martin's hockey programme, these changes would present huge cultural, religious and sporting challenges. For a start, English, yes English, in this part of London's heartland, was becoming the second language to Urdu.

Yet, to 'The Fox', that was academic, because hockey was the Boss. By then in the mid-90s, his coaching, training and ferrying boys around the dark streets of Hackney and Bethnal Green had made hockey a full-time occupation. His junior team led by Jagdish Barbar, Abdul Kahar and Shuhel Ullah were Anglo-Bengalis, but were steeped in the Asian style. Martin even once convinced the Pakistan National team to come down to Homerton and play his young charges. Score? Not at all bad, 1-4 to the Pakistan Team!

Nevertheless, there now was a difference. Despite winning several National Under16 titles with outstanding merit, the families of these Bengalis wanted their sons to be upwardly mobile, to aim for the professions, to be doctors, lawyers and businessmen in the City. In short, these first generation migrants were more like Alan Sugar than Nicky Thompson. Just like Nicky, they loved playing the game, but their eyes were set long time on a different direction. How many, though clearly talented enough, went on to play for England, the full England side or the Olympic team?

The answer was none. It was a cultural issue. Their loyalty was first and foremost to their family and religion, but with a drive to go up through the levels of British life. They could never see hockey as a means to achieving that. It is a fact that England Hockey never understood them, and never backed the hockey pros that had an affiliation to such groups from such backgrounds. Just ask yourself was Soma Singh or Julian Halls used in later life to foster the brilliant job that The Fox had devoted his lifetime to? It was repeated all over the urban areas of Birmingham and Manchester, such a waste of talent.

Equally over the last 15 years, Hackney is beginning to rise from the ashes. The former single sex enclaves of schools have been terminated and replaced by spanking new colours and shapes of buildings. New government schemes, beginning with central government intervening by setting up "The Learning Trust" for Hackney in 2000 to stimulate learning, curriculum and community. The Borough has received huge investment into the formation of Academies, coeducation with uniforms and a move towards more modern teaching methods with a full range of ICT facilities and specialised colleges, including special needs educational centres. Lottery finance at primary level through the Sure Start programme is now starting to make an impact in addition to GCSE attainment much improved. Over a decade period, Hackney secured over £5 million in capital investment which did not include the £8 million for Sure Start and nursery schemes.

Homerton House was knocked down in 2005 as part of this renewal policy and replaced by the City Academy. Bulging out expansively with modern architectural design, it fronts up to the future. Where the playground of uneven bounce and sloping profile used to be, is now a state of the art rubber crumb synthetic surface, testimony to a practical sporting provision. The ghosts of Homerton hockey, Gladman, Ashton, Jagdish, Ehiogu, Kahah, and Thompson are now but spooks from the past, but they lie in the very fabric of that Homerton home.

What of the privileged ones just up on the Olympic stadium level looking down the Homerton Road from the distance? Look? I doubt that England Hockey's beautiful people even give Hackney a cursory glance. Why, indeed, should they? They never have.

Has it ever occurred to them that the thirty years before their gift from the Olympic movement, there were dozens and dozens of young, brilliant hockey players that were educated in the harshest of environments. More poignantly, while they clap each other on the back dishing out gongs and OBEs to their lovely ladies, do they not realise that they have never rewarded or recognised the man that made it all happen beside those Marshes.

That man, the guru of junior hockey was and is "The Fox", Martin Foxall, the living embodiment of Hackney's Mission Statement, "A good place to grow up."

High rise backdrop to "The Patch".

'Last orders for Fitz' – The Highwayman SW15

'* * * * BASHING'
ON COMMON
—COURT STORY

TWELVE youths, 11 from Roehampton and the other from Barnes, were alleged at the Old Bailey on Monday to have paid a late night visit to Wimbledon Common.

After arming themselves with wooden staves they lay in ambush near a pedestrian subway which led on to the common. When a suitable victim came along he was beaten about the head and face and left dying outside the gates of Putney Vale Cemetery, said Mr. Leary.

Boy gets
life
sentence

'Attacked * * * *' was
left 'like a jigsaw
puzzle'—story

The boys hit the local and national headlines.

Top striker in the Hoofdklasse – Simon Egerton at H.C.Rotterdam.

the kid from 'Acknee' done well – Nick Thompson, England and GB.

Homerton Home. All in, the cops and community officers as well!

'The Fox' with Homerton House at half-time. "He took us off the streets and gave us real values".

Ali Ghazanfar receives his Champions Trophy medal for Pakistan, the ultimate professional.

Bernhard Peters, top of the hockey coaching world, now at Hamburg S.V. the guru of football academies.

The incomparable Wagener Stadion in Amstelveen, full to the brim as usual.

Full to capacity at the Indoor World Cup finals in Berlin.

Andy Mair in pulsating form as Britain's greatest umpire.

Along with astroturf, has any one element influenced modern hockey as much as the video camera?

Chapter 13

When Hockey Met Footey

The Director of Sport for Premier Bundesliga Club Hamburg SV perused the scene at the Volksparkstadion from his office window high up amongst a multitude of club workers. To his right was the brand new Academy Sports centre building surrounded by two new cork-filled Astroturf surfaces designed for fussball. Below him, on the floor below, was the beginnings of a commercial trade fair attracting companies from all over Germany motivated to become involved with Hamburg SV.

He had reached the top of his trade, and as he journeyed along the corridor, the proof of such attainment was the reminder of the great personalities that had also been a part of this great European football club; the likes of Uwe Seeler, Manfred Kaltz and the celebrated Englander Kevin Keegan were portrayed proudly along the walls.

For Bernhard Peters has occupied an essential role in modern football, that of supervising junior development at the club since 2014. For those of us that have held the view that the term 'development' precludes the word 'achievement' better quickly think again. With this native from the small border village of Rheine in Nordrhein Westfalen, he had shattered any distinct separation of the two words.

From the wise saying, 'What goes around, comes around' was ironically telling for Bernhard. He returned to his office to pinch himself of the reminder that all that surrounded him was real. After all, it was all so different from his origins of watching as a teenager his local provincial team, Die Fohlen (The Foals) of Borussia Mönchengladbach back in the 1970s. Bernhard's first real introduction to team sports was watching, in his case observing, the successful way that Hennes Weisweiler had for the entire decade produced such a fast, exciting brand of football.

In short, Bernhard was hooked. He was to witness how Hennes would manage the intense rivalry of his German legends like Jupp Heynckes, Günter Netzer and Bertie Vogts contesting Bundesliga crowns against Bayern Munich's Beckenbauer, Muller and Breitner. These were halcyon days for German football.

Perhaps what really impressed the young Bernhard was not just the team efficiency but its undying passion for fast open play. Yet, could it last, he asked himself; would this golden generation continue beyond the seven or eight years of its elevation? Maybe, just maybe, that was the club's Achilles heel.

Again ironically, the young coach in Bernhard would not at this stage find the answer to that question within the borders of Deutschland. It would invisibly reveal itself to him from one match between his beloved Borussia and the 'Beatles' music city of Liverpool in May of 1973. The game was the UEFA two legged final, and from the first leg at Anfield, Liverpool had built an unassailable three goal lead. It was the two-man strike strike force of John Toschack and Kevin Keegan that combined to allow the future Hamburg hero Keegan to score two and have a penalty kick saved!

Liverpool F.C., having been a potent force since the early 1960s, were to extend their dominance through the subsequent two decades which included a 1977 European Cup Final win against Borussia after Keegan had departed for Germany. At that stage, it was still very doubtful that a young Bernhard had even heard of the Liverpool 'Boot Room'. Yet, it was the very method orchestrated by the original manager Bill Shankly that would be mirrored down through the years of Bernhard Peters's coaching.

To define the 'Boot Room' would not only be the description of 'the Liverpool Way' of playing over three decades, but rather how it was implemented by a succession of team coaches across the football club. Bill Shankly had brought together a diverse group of successful practitioners under one roof to take charge of a method of play, and protect that approach whomever was officially the Head Coach. Initially across his organisation was Bob Paisley, Joe Fagan, Ronnie Moran and Roy Evans. Five coordinators to cover the club's 1st, 2nd, Apprentice and Schoolboy teams made their whole very well defined. First team and Head Coach Shankly pulled the strings up until 1974, with Paisley succeeding him for nigh on the next decade, who gave way later on to Fagan and Evans.

They all had served their 'apprenticeship' with each other and by each other. Their structural basis was both autocratic and democratic. The actual 'Boot Room', a ramshackle devoted space of sawdust and rickety benches as seats did exist with a minimum number of plug points to make the tea as background refreshment to their weekly deliberations. Their combined preparations and analysis really would have been worth recording, but initiatives, assessments, and post-match debriefs were shared to combined debate.

Thus, each component of the club was open to interest and interpretation–a problem shared was a problem solved across the club's teams. As mentioned earlier, their quest was for achievement and development at the same time, and over the long term of three decades. The great majority of players during this period were either home grown or very carefully scouted by the likes of Ronnie Moran. Club achievement was manifested in a record number of English League Championships, European and UEFA Cup wins with a variety of generations of players, but more to the point was the transfer of junior level success into their players of the future to win senior titles.

Youth development was the key to it all. By the time Bernhard Peters was to leave home in Rheine to attend the famous Sports School in Köln to study physical education, he had by a very tender age realised that after being a junior hockey club member at Krefeld Hockey Club, he really had derived as much fulfilment from helping and guiding others in the sport as he did from playing! His parents were from the merchant sector of employment with scant inclination to teach or coach. Nevertheless, it was through his observation of football, and his inspiration from how Weisweiler had organised the Mönchengladbach teams that had made him realise that football and hockey coaching could be easily transferable.

His tenure in Köln was to expose him not only to the practical knowledge of teaching the physical elements of several sports, but also to read the literature and absorb the specialised lectures from a variety of hockey experts based in the area and at the School. He was in a stimulating environment with senior personnel including Hugo Budinger and Klaus Kleiter, who he was later to work with as a coaching assistant in the Deutsche Hockey-Bund. In late 70s German hockey, Bernhard had also read the pioneering books from Horst Wein, who by then had become the National Coach of Spain.

This concentration of hockey talent had spread to the success of the Köln clubs, Swartz and Rot-Weiss and their climb to the top of national club hockey with gold medal Olympian Michel Krause and indoor icon Wolfgang Hillman. Absorbed by all these positive influences, by graduation day Bernhard was sold on a career in hockey. He had all the tools and motivation, then at that stage was his opportunity to earn his spurs at club level. He knew he could achieve that by returning to Krefeld, his home club.

Still, what interested him most was working with young players and seeing their daily progress in acquiring not just technical proficiency, but also in their understanding of the tactical elements that enriched the expanding sport. He saw development of the player as the direct route to individual and team success, and it was here in West Germany that he would prosper in hockey terms as a result of his adherence to the 'Boot Room' association of achievement through development. He was never aware of the events transpiring in Liverpool. His was very much a German progression with the knowledge that success would bring him individual opportunity. That was the German way!

Before any cohesive action along the lines of the 'Boot Room' could be envisaged, it was essential for Bernhard to plough his own furrow, and there would be no better place than the low division Krefeld in men's and women's hockey. The club would be his proving ground. After all, with the ideas he had formulated, why practise them on a top Bundesliga club like Mulheim or at the Köln clubs? His leaning towards developing players and their understanding on unit play had the potential to massively improve team play and, thus, progression up the leagues.

In other words, achievement followed development, and in his case the two were almost inseparable as they ran so quickly together. Little did Coach Peters realise at this stage that he was planting the seeds of much greater things to come. He knew that, for instance, 'the best training exercises were written by the match'.

He never needed to spoon-feed the players to improve their decision-making powers. Here his use of video management was paramount–he advocated coaches to observe video, and reproduce those exact field situations to repetitive training practices. That way the player could recognise and identify, individually or in a group session, the game decision required. The coach presents the picture; the players attach the brush strokes.

Bernhard strongly advanced the ideas of players working within sub-units of the field spatially. He knew there was little point in such a world-class striker as Oliver Domke training for deep defensive left-hand-side unit play. Nevertheless, units such as right-hand-side systematic wide play, structured integrated backline defence and even sixteen-yard hit out options were areas he put great concentration upon to push the players' theoretical and practical understanding of the game.

Anyone watching a Bernhard Peters's team was in no doubt that they had definition in distinct areas of the field. Krefeld were no exception as they accelerated up the leagues to top Bundesliga play. By the end of the 80s, and at the tender age of 27, his Krefeld women's team was attracting widespread attention and Coach Peters was duly appointed by the D.H.B. to head up the coaching team at the inaugural U21 Junior Women's World Cup in Ottawa in 1989, and, you've already guessed it–Bernhard began his love affair with the World Cup event by guiding the girls to gold at his first attempt!

Hockey in the late 80s was beginning to embrace the assets presented by sports medicine, and Herr Peters was at the forefront of this vanguard. He expected video analysis, specific athletic training, and the role that could be played by exponents from other sports. Indeed, with the Köln lecture group environment, students specialising in teaching football at Head Courses were being instructed by hockey trainers. It cut both ways, did expertise.

So, in his early years at the D.H.B., Bernhard was gaining vital strides ahead of his Australian, New Zealander, British and Spanish counterparts in the support sections to hockey. In addition, as he was moving on to the German Men's U21 group for the 90s decade, he knew he needed to master the Asian game. It was here where the Germans stole a march on their rivals by in-depth studies on the fundamentals of the Asian style, notably by sending the full delegation of coaches to tournaments played in Asia.

A full delegation meant Senior Coach Paul Lissek, U21's supremo Bernhard and the German U18 coaching staff as well, working together in analysis on the ground. Remind you of somewhere? Please note now that in the decade between 1993 and the Olympics in 2004, Bernhard as the U21 coach won one gold and one bronze. Moving on to the senior level at the millennium, he guided Germany to gold in 2002 and 2006 at World Cup level. In addition, Olympic gold, silver and bronzes were achieved at men and women's level during this consistently successful time.

It sounds like the list of Liverpool F.C.'s achievements in the 70s and 80s and, with good reason, Bernhard described this parallel interconnection between the age group coaches as the 'Common Red Line'. Lissek, with Peters and Markus Weise, had effectively produced their cohesive Deutsche 'Boot Room'.

There can be no doubt that, from Kleiter to Weise, in a period of a quarter of a century, that the four men served nearly a hundred years as head coaches within the organisation, stressing the need of continuity and evolution, but most of all, as coaches they were a team within a team. Bernhard was never one to cross-refer to other nations, but he hinted that in many other formative hockey nations there was not enough broad consensus between the age group and gender group coaches and coaching methodology. This was where the Germans had the trump card, as success invariably bred success.

After such achievements from the development of players through the age group teams, it became inevitable that internal German 'spies' were carefully assessing and admiring the work done in national hockey, and by Bernhard as the major link in the chain over the preceding decade and a half. They were from football, and from newly appointed head coach, Jurgen Klinsmann, in 2004. He had approached Bernhard in discussions to initiate a Sports Director for the D.F.B., the national organisation.

Their broad agreement to move him from hockey to football utilising many of the hockey men's exceptional principles and methodology was mutually enthusiastic, but the concept of that innovation was lost at that time on some of football's administrators. In short, they were not quite ready for a hockey man to be considered for a perceived number one spot! Integrating junior and senior coaching ideas, ensuring a cohesive approach between the clubs and the country, and, most of all, harnessing methods from another sport, was still just a wee bit radical. Never forget, that in nations like England, Australia and India, these concepts had hardly got off the ground, full stop!

If the national German football authorities were not quite ready yet, the clubs certainly were, and in a sporting swoop, Bernhard grabbed the headlines in 2006 by being appointed as the first Sporting Director with special responsibilities to junior development at F.C. Hoffenheim. Hoffen who?, you might say, were a third division amateur club that had recently benefited from the return to the Heidelberg area of software mogul Dietmar Hopp as a financial backer. Yet, it was really only after 2006 and Bernhard's arrival that his investments, financial and in personnel, were beginning to promote the club towards professionalism and a Bundesliga status in 2008.

There was quite some resentment and criticism of the Hopp regime from the point of view of purists that this newly promoted club from a village backwater of less than 4,000 people held no traditions in the sport. The often-quoted phrase, 'they would be here today and gone tomorrow', always hung over the administrators and coaching staff alike. Yet Hopp was shrewd enough as the club's fortunes gained ground to bring medium-term stability with the appointment of an experienced Bundesliga Manager in Ralf Rangnick.

Like Bernhard as Sports Director, he was offered a five-year contract, a medium-term commitment that could have the time to lay down the foundation blocks of linking junior development with senior achievement. So even with the envy of the critics of such clubs like Hoffenheim, which suffered similar experiences of vitriol as Bayer Leverkusen and Wolfsburg faced as big company sponsored teams, the first team stabilised for a number of years.

Bernhard Peters, the hockey coach, was quietly working behind the scenes to build up the youth wing and hit relatively early success in 2008 as German National U17 Champions, but would these players go on to senior success? After Rangnick left at the end of 2010, the club had four different managers in just two years. Coach Peters's 'Common Red Line' had been broken by the instability at senior management level. However, there was some recovery with the appointment of Markus Gisdol in 2013 for three seasons, during which the U19 team became German national champions and runners-up in two successive seasons. Again, it was only proving Bernhard's firm belief that stability and cohesion was, in coaching terms, the bedrock of all the teams within the club.

By 2014, not only had he built two connective academies within Hoffenheim, he had laid the foundation of his youth teams that would progress to the fourth place that the club occupies today in 2018 in the Bundesliga. He had done the hard yards as the transition from one sport, hockey, had proven the football experts wrong. More than this, he had shown the team coaching fraternity that, with a tried and tested methodology, development was the twin brother of achievement.

Within football and hockey fields for so long, why had they been so separate? Fans out there may disagree, but you can surely only claim that Ferguson, Mourinho in football and Charlesworth and Reteuggi in hockey were achievers, but did they develop players? Once a close-knit generation retired, they either hit the cheque book or the large numbers of available players from elsewhere.

On the other hand, the 'developers' in the two sports have the distinction of consistently achieving. That was not the case with Arsene Wegner or former England manager Ron Greenwood. Wenger in 22 years never won a European trophy as the ultimate European citizen! In hockey, David Vinson and Bert Bunnik did sterling work as directors of coaching principles, but they seldom were described as serial achievers.

It has been the German coaches who are the exception to this rule, with Horst Wein and Paul Lissek extending their medal count to working in the development spheres of hockey and football coaching respectively in Latin

America and Asia. They escaped the comfort zone of FIH and FIFA rule books to work independently of national borders and organisations.

Bernhard, however, remains at the top of the pile. Whether it has been training male or female players, whether it has been junior U21 or seniors, and whether it has been small unfashionable clubs or International World Champions, he has been at the forefront of the understanding of core principles to teams and individuals alike. The very fact that he was able to move from one Olympic sport to another world game speaks volumes in itself.

The most recent move took him from Hoffenheim to the port city of Hamburg, where after four years he has established his priorities as Director of Sport at Hamburg SV. One of Germany's giant clubs with a huge fan base around the world, he has had to confront new challenges as globalisation has affected this cash-rich sport in such a short period. His academy sector has tentacles into many parts of Africa and new 'player markets' for teenagers in China.

His team of coaches are now, thus, world-travelled, passing on through clinics and scouting Bernhard's aspirations for Hamburg. Already, his players from the Academy are graduating to senior levels of Bundesliga football more numerous than any other club in Germany with training methods at the forefront of modern technology.

Yet, as Bernhard is still facing up to football's challenging evolution, he still glances over his shoulder, smiles and thinks of the sport he left behind, but still is very much in his blood. He sits back in his cathedral of a stadium and assesses how hockey is experimenting with nine and five players, with restrictive numbers to occupy certain sectors of the pitch, setting basketball time quarters, and three 'points' for a field goal!

Does he miss hockey? He responds, 'It is not my time in hockey anymore. It seems the sport has overreacted to the International Olympic Committee's pressure on its Olympic inclusion. Hockey is producing radical solutions to non-existent problems.' If anyone can be an authority worldwide on this matter, he must be up there with the best from Olympic hockey and commercial football.

'Football is the success it is, because it is a simple game. It has never compromised on its identity, hockey must do the same.'

Bernhard, 'Wir stimme zu!'

Chapter 14

Last Tango in Paris

Édith Neppit trooped off the Merignac field soaked to the skin. Another Atlantic storm had battered the Aquitaine region of the South-West as was its custom at the beginning of January. She had also been subjected to another equally tough midweek training session to prepare her National League team for the competition in the second half of the season. These sessions were based on physical fitness. Édith was a technical player and to her mind, she did not need nor want physical pain from hockey.

Tuesday evenings slog up and down Merignac's one 'Astro' surface were exacerbated by the rush off to work afterwards at her night shift at La Tribune, a 45-minute drive away across the teeming traffic of Bordeaux. For the entire journey she had weighed up the value of playing and training for hockey to play each weekend in the distant parts of France at such an average level.

It was all starting to interfere with a very promising journalist career at 'The Tribune'. After successfully receiving a distinction as a student at L'Institut de Journalisme in Bordeaux, she had landed a plum role at the 'Daily' as an assistant Editor and reporter under the tutelage of the sports legend, Antoine Le Boeuf. She could speak openly with him and this time, she'd inform him that it was time to pack in hockey and make herself available for further duties and advancement at the paper.

Antoine was old school through and through, a meat and potatoes man who had cut his teeth in the late twentieth century as a young sports reporter. He was part of the pen and notepad gossip generation that understood deadlines and the need for the public to know the story behind the lurid headlines. After three decades at the sharp end, Antoine now, with a widening girth and a slightly jaundiced tinge to his complexion after years on the dreaded 'Gauloises', was within five years of early retirement to his retreat in the Dordogne.

As a young man he loved anything connected with sport, knew the game as a player of rugby union inside out, and yes, as a reporter had shared a 'bouteille' or two with the greats from Serge Blanco to Jonnie Wilkinson. Nevertheless, only one area for him eclipsed the rugby field and that was 'Les Jeux d'Olympiques'. He claimed ownership of the world's greatest sporting theatre to his proud homeland after Baron De Coubertin had innovated its inception over a hundred years ago. In short, Antoine was a walking encyclopaedia for all things Olympic.

Moreover, when Paris was awarded the Games for 2024, one hundred years after the 1924 event in the capital, he gave all his journalist workers a party day off in the Médoc to celebrate on a claret-inspired mystery bus tour!

Just as Édith was preparing her news for Antoine, he interrupted,

"By now, Édie, you must be tired of covering the mundane. I can see it in your face every time you venture out to the next rugby game, gymnastics Festival or volleyball tourney. You have earned your spurs, now you must gravitate to some sports investigative journalism and explore the guts of sport."

So far so good, Édith thought, music to her ears!

"I want you, ma belle, to venture out to compile a complete assessment of the state of Olympic sports just five to six years prior to the Games in Paris. Our readers need to know the state of play, and what is happening with the leading sports here in France and internationally in their preparations for the great show. They want to know the ins and outs, the movers and shakers, their 'raison d'être'. Our little rag here will be the source of all things Olympic. Today, the Tribune, tomorrow the great National and International News Moguls."

"I will provide you with the contacts and you will run all over Europe to deliver the goods on three sports per year until 2024. I will okay your finished product after you have interviewed the real personalities, but there will be great opportunities for your own editorial comment and analysis. Can you hack it? You will start next Monday with Men and Women's Hockey. I think you already know a thing or two about Le Hockey sur Gazon!!?

"On a practical level, Antoine, will I be relieved of my statutory duties and hours of work here at the offices?" Édie enquired.

"Yes, from now on, you are project based, you can work from home and utilise all the professional help and facilities at 'The Tribune'. I just need you to set up a weekly time for the two of us for ongoing progress reports. All expenses, travel, hotels, research acquisitions, you can deal with in the normal way."

Antoine expressly voiced a desire to know which events Édie would cover in 2018, prompting her to combine interviews simultaneously at competitions and tournaments, notably in the international arena, and to try where possible to make combined assessment of men and women's hockey together as one package. It was decided at an early stage that she would designate the Indoor World Cup in Berlin, the European Men's Hockey League and the Women's World Cup in London as her major targets for collaborative meetings with personnel from Asia, Africa, North America, Australia and of course Europe.

The FIH officials, based in Europe, would inevitably be in attendance at these focal points as world representatives meeting at Committee level during the tournaments. As for France, she would be using her hockey connections and be available in an ongoing capacity during the next six months as an observer of the Élite League and play-offs.

Édie was delighted at the prospect of such work, and was very well equipped to involve herself in the more international side of liaison with foreign nationals. She had indeed herself spent her gap year between school and the University Institute playing for a London club side, and never forget, she had been selected for the National French Under 18 women's team as a very promising central defender. However, that was before her more than social three years at the Institute and the pressurised two-year cooker of working under a more than demanding Antoine. Her hockey had suffered alarmingly with the coaching staff at Merignac struggling to get her in shape for top club level hockey. Frankly, she was not fit for purpose.

Now, she was out of that, and very soon her contacts would be setting up fact-finding missions with hockey exponents from Pakistan, Holland, Germany, the USA, Australia and Southern Africa. She was to meet managers, coaches, administrators, umpires and most of all, players. Some would be forthright and others anonymous, because as she was to discover, hockey in 2018 was a very political game, and more poignantly, a sport in turmoil.

She would first infiltrate the umbrella body that controlled the sport, the Federation of International Hockey, and the main reason for that objective was that the French Federation would have to work closely with them as an organisation if the 2024 Olympic tournament was to be a success. She did find insecurity and turmoil, and it all followed down from an IOC meeting in February 2013 as a target committee drew up a list of five sports to be considered for elimination from the Games of the future. Hockey, to the shock of the FIH, was one of them – the others were Taekwondo, Modern

Pentathlon, Synchronised Swimming and Wrestling. The remit was to axe two in the recommendation stage.

Hockey survived by the skin of its teeth, but it rocked the glitterati of a new young officialdom which had become very Anglicised since the hockey tournament's success in London in 2012. The modern group of university trained professionals in Sport had moved in under the well-respected Leandro Negri from Spain to control the sport through to Rio in 2016. The IOC target group's message was clear, adapt or die! With over 1200 hockey athletes and officials in search of only six medals, the sport was too numerous, and as Édith already knew, it was dominated in men and women's hockey by The Netherlands, Germany and Australia, the developed world.

The IOC wanted diversity, inclusivity, gender equality and thrills and spills in sport, that were easy to understand, and most essential, could be directed by live streaming through the television networks and their unassailable connect to sponsors and big money. It had become a race to the top of a monied pile.

Édith knew that she had a problem gaining candid interviews and putting names to faces. She trolled over the next two months the club evenings of London, the offices of Germany and the pubs like the 1890 outside the Amstelveen stadium, but all she met were comments like, "Don't quote me" and "this is off the record." The family of hockey had become introspective, suspicious and worst of all, was that these features compounded its already established elite reputation that the IOC was palpably not impressed with.

So she took the notes, filled the books but was more convinced every day to record their actions, what the FIH were actually doing to change the game and how genuine hockey people were reacting to the decisions from up above.

Inside the field were the incessant number of rule changes. She wondered how the Umpires kept up with the self-start free hit, the edge of circle attacking free hit traffic flow, no long corners but more free hits opposite where the ball went out, own goals, and at International level, 4×15 minute quarter time periods and the intrusion of a Video Umpire!! If that was not bad enough, the Euro Hockey League now were issuing pocket calculators as a new 'points' system of three from open play and only one for a penalty corner, resulted in one game result of: –

Bloemendaal 15 Arminem 2!!

Mademoiselle Nippet, a French patriot, pulled into the railway station in London that was named after the demise of her Napoleonic homeland, Waterloo! She was, however, to meet a true son of the 'auld' enemy, from Scotland, Andy Mair. He had been at the forefront of the FIH over the preceding decade as a leading world umpire at the majors and the newly innovated competitions of the European Hockey and India Hockey Leagues. They retired upstairs for a glass or two of claret with Édith noting that Antoine would well approve.

"Well, what is your reaction to the FIH wanting Pro 9 League World Series and the host of changes within the rules?"

"Let's differentiate between the new dynamic rules and the changing competition structures, even though that evolution is motivated by and for the same ends. The rules can always be a problem in that they can be very positive measures for the top end of play, but sometimes can be incompatible to apply to the grassroots, e.g. the abolition of the 'Long Corner' to 25 yard Free Hits, and the time change to four fifteen minute quarters.

Having accepted that, like the self-start hits and the more liberal interpretations on feet, obstruction and the lifted ball, the FIH have rightly used the EHL and IHL as good areas of experimentation with the aim of speeding up the game and make it more attractive on the eye. We are in a TV dominated spectator world which demands detailed analysis and fairness, hence the use of VAR, the Video Assisted 'Referee'. Whatever the diverse reaction to it in other sports, it has proved to be a positive agent in enhancing the game and producing equanimity.

The product has to be simple and we have fine-tuned the relationship between fast play, replay and slow motion and between the timing of our VAR in his box and the crowd at large with the emphasis on retaining the flow and continuity of the game. In short, we are three strides ahead of football. Televising by 2024 in Paris we should have a précised finished product.

That is why 'Indoor Hockey' is such a hit with the television gurus because there is close-knit interaction between players, coaches, umpires and the spectators. Everything is close to the action interdependent on each other. Just remember, Édith, you were in Berlin, what a marvellous spectacle with nigh on 10,000 people in such a tightly enclosed arena. It was electric, and what must be relevant for you in France was the contribution and quality that the unfavoured nations like Iran, Belarus and Namibia brought to the Indoor World Cup Finals finishing 3rd, 4th and 9th respectively.

The fast nature of skilled enclosed 6-a-side hockey was appreciated by the fervent fans, the Television Companies and the FIH, so keen to showcase the diverse nature of the Hockey Family in Asia, Africa and the Americas."

Édith paused, and then asked the ultimate question,

"Why, Andy, are we so dominated by the IOC, pushing us to make these ridiculous radical changes like nine aside and the Pro nine League, an elitist paradise, when we already have the indoor game?

"We know we are under threat by the IOC as a potentially excluded sport. I am not sure if that is such a bad thing as there are many major world sports that are not part of the Olympics. Why change the fabric of our team sport, which still ironically at the Olympics is watched by more spectators than any other, apart from Athletics!" he added.

"Antoine would turn in his grave! Maybe not, as long as hockey was replaced by Rugby Sevens!!" Édith mused.

And he concluded by informing her that over the last five years, there was serious consideration to move hockey to the Winter Olympics as an indoor sport with the perceived positive action. The only minus point being the lack of participation in the hotter underdeveloped world of Africa and Asia. Yet, it is still on the 'front burner'.

"Paris could yet be the last Olympics for field hockey! That may well be beyond the powers of you guys in France!"

She was cognisant of everything Andy threw at her having been in Berlin and witnessed such a hockey success of an indoor tournament. Whilst there, she had met German players and officials alike who simply pointed at the Court with its stands of spectators encircling the playing arena almost touching points and insisted,

"This game is the future for the Olympics! It is easy to have an appreciation, it is very televisual and for the National Associations it is much more affordable to build and maintain long-term."

On this second trip in March to Europe, she was keen enough to have postponed a few meetings with Antoine until she had organised a series of consultations with players and coaches from Holland and the visiting observer from the USA of the European Hockey League Qualifiers. Just 1km from the Wagener Stadium in Amstelveen is the infamous Hockey Hotel, the

Abina, a more than festive three-storey resting and partying venue for all hockey fans and devotees visiting this hockey mecca.

Hockey men and women funnelled into the spacious bar to debate along with a touring Club coach from Philadelphia, Jon Williams. He had been a stalwart of internal nation team training in leagues as diverse as New Zealand, Portugal, England and now the USA's. The Dutch lads and lasses wanted to remain anonymous but let it be said, there were Hoofdklasse players present from Amsterdam and Rotterdam.

"How do you fit in all these differing demands on you, as some of you are not even full-time hockey pros?" Édith asked.

A leading light represented all the views by stating you have to go full-time. "We deeply believe in club hockey and in National and European competition. Our standards as high as they are, must be retained as the best League for clubs in the World. Just look who took the Olympic medals in Rio in 2016, the nations with strong club traditions. The Men were Argentina, Belgium and Germany and with the women, GB, Holland and Germany. Hockey does not need Pro nines and the World Series; they are just wasted air miles, too expensive to sustain in the long term, and they will kill the players."

Jon Williams agreed;

"My experience in the English National League is similar with sport at elite level asking athletes to play games and train back to back six times per week when you include club, indoor and the demands of the National squad. That is why in 2008 we had the birth of full-time hockey, and Club England was to pay the players' bills. Now, factor in the FIH schedule of international India HL, the EHL, Indoor tournaments and the Pro 9 and you have ultimate congestion. What will suffer?"

To Jon's mind, it would be quality in a heap of fatigue. He just could not believe that the FIH would cower to these crazy (a word that Andy Mair also associated with the expanded programme) demands set by ambitious interests on the periphery or outside the sport. He continued with the Dutch players ironically enjoying the real fruits of the Hockey family in the very appropriate background of the sounds and festive atmosphere of the one and only Abina Hotel.

By May, Édith was back in the office facing the penetrating stare of Le Boeuf. She retorted how the world of hockey had grown, but like a patch of weeds, had overgrown. Riddled with vested interests within the FIH, from Australia's "don't forget us" radical solutions of crazy tampering with the sport's identity, dimensions and numbers, to the cosy elite of the English inspired inner circles, the confusion was mind-boggling. She reported the truth on the temporary nature of the FIH personnel.

"You know Antoine, from the World Cup in 2014, their Development group of President Leandro Negri, CEO Kelly Fairweather, his Assistant Mike Joyce, Guru marketeers Richard Tattershaw with David Luckes and Sarah Massey had touted their "Hockey Revolution" through to the 2016 Olympics. By the end of that year, they had all resigned or had terminated their tenure! All of them, gone! Not one there to implement their great plans for the new World order."

Antoine puffed on his Gauloise, exhorting the Gallic shrug of his shoulders, saying, "They are all the same, their careers are their focus, not the sport. C'est la vie!"

Forgetting them, Antoine was more concerned about the future of hockey at the Olympics, emotionally rejecting Andy Mair's relatively ambivalent report on the dubious necessity for the sport to be tied to the hip with the Olympic movement.

"The five rings are sacrosanct, and hockey for a hundred years has been at the forefront of the Olympic creed, it must continue, especially on our watch in 2024."

"For us in France, we need the living spirit of the Games and the embodiment of the entertainment it can bring to our people that play hockey. Stuff Europeans, what about the Asians, the true exponents of skills and thrills, and the colour and freedom that the Africans can bring to the Turf. Édith, go out and assess where they are in this sport, before us focusing on hockey within our borders."

Édith was able to catch up just before a coaching assignment in Oman with the respected and well-travelled Pakistan player and coach, Ali Ghazanfar at Schiphol airport in Amsterdam. She asked,

"Ali, so what is the state of the Asian game?

"We have essentially a kit bag full of troubles in Pakistan from the huge changes in our schools curriculum where hockey has been taken out of the traditional day-to-day practice to, of course, the national security of our country in terms of potential terrorism. Édith, you know it does not do our standing any good in world respect when the FIH propose our future home games in the Pro-League in of all places, Scotland!

"For us, for some time, India has been a thorn in our side as the FIH have fully supported their cause through the hosting of continued numbers of FIH Champions Trophies and World Cups as we suffer as their neighbour with no internal development or external encouragement. Our standards have slipped, a factor that our predecessors (we call them the class of '84) constantly remind us undermining any revival. As for India with huge numbers of Dutch and Australasian "experts" helping their cause, they are going around and around in circles, still not breaking into the top six in Senior World hockey.

Our cousins in Malaysia and Korea have also subsequently experienced the decline in playing numbers that has been a direct result of globalisation as they have both become exposed to other world games like football, motorsports and basketball. The buzz for hockey that Antoine's generation experienced from Asian teams is not there anymore with many omissions from World Cup finals. You must tell him it is a question today of whether Asian teams can qualify for the Olympics."

It was the same story from Africa. Lack of funds, and isolation from the modern aspects of sports medicine and full-time players have resulted in an uneven playing field with the full-time pros of North West Europe and Australasia competing at Olympic events with nations like Spain, Egypt, South Africa and Pakistan where the money and expertise had dried up. The FIH had not helped.

Édith's knowledge was virtually complete as she had come to some interesting conclusions for France to take stock of, even before her presentation to Antoine.

Later that summer in 2018, Antoine received her report, and it was positive. There was a real sense of purpose and motivation in her writing, and enthusiasm that even spilled over into her own appearance as she was looking trimmer and brighter. This, despite her findings within the FIH and the evident fracturing of the hockey family at international, competitive level. She had in her travels still found that the grassroots of the game where social integration with the competitive spirit, notably in clubs, was alive and kicking. She had recommended that France could and should look at Argentina, a fellow 'Latin' country as a role model in its approach to the sport.

Yes, Belgium now ranked 3rd or 4th in the men's game had moulded a Dutch approach to push their game forward to new heights, but it was in the centralised concentration of hockey in Buenos Aires (the Paris of South America in many respects) with its huge outlying provinces as in France that could lead the way to how her country could perform well in 2024 and establish the template to expand the game domestically from that pinnacle.

"Let's face it Antoine, hockey in France is undersubscribed, never in the Press, seldom on TV and played by very small numbers around the country. The regions are bereft of development or talent in the sport and the distances between Lille, Nice, Bretagne and here in Aquitaine are too great for any regular playing or coaching interactions. There are few clubs, and notably there are often only two teams like I experienced at Merignac in the entire club, and we were in the French Premier Division.

The coaching structure is virtually non-existent in all regions with Senior men's players adopting the role. We literally have a brain drain to Paris. Our top young players are directed to Paris through education and then having studied there, settle in the capital city. You cannot believe it, Antoine, it is so disheartening."

"Ah, mais oui," he interjected, "Our Parisian clubs in the men are improving at a fast rate, you saw it yourself, Racing Club and St. Germain have made big inroads in the European Hockey League."

"Yes true, but it's only the same two teams every year that tend to contest our National finals. The sport cannot survive off those two teams alone, and God help the women where we are nowhere in numbers nor in the European Clubs League."

Antoine knew also about the dependency on local authorities and singular benefactors to support these clubs in their existence to survive. The majority of regional clubs were playing on facilities that they had to share with other sports like football. Other clubs were bankrolled by rich patriarchs who were more intent on upholding the rich social life with a culinary life second to none, but a severe blank on competition and achievement.

They agreed, in 2024, it would have to be Paris versus the World at the Olympics, but was that so different from London representing Great Britain, or more pertinently, Buenos Aires upholding the fortunes of Argentina? There had to be a centralisation programme for the Olympics to work for France, whether it was an in-house residential scheme entirely, or some kind of release system from the clubs of Racing, Stade Francais, St. Germain and Montrouge to the National squad. Both ideas could work.

Édith submitted her report by hand that day to Antoine even before the forthcoming Women's World Cup in July in London. It was still only May and she was showing all the joys of spring. Antoine received the full download, and would study it in detail later that week, but there was unusually a preface in the shape of a request from the author. The attachment simply asked leave of absence from June to October.

The shock hit Antoine immediately demanding an explanation after he had given the young woman such a journalistic role with such flexibility. Édith now wanted out, but only temporarily, and out of the country for four months.

"Is this a female thing, are you in some kind of trouble, I can't think why, you're looking in great shape?"

Édith laughed and simply stated

"Yes, Antoine, it is a female thing, I want to be far away from France to continue my Olympic research – in Buenos Aires, Argentina in a practical manner by playing for one of the city's premier clubs."

"I knew there was something, you have been training, you are in great shape n'est-ce pas?"

Édith had rekindled her passion for the sport whilst conducting her work those last three months, even enrolling with a personal trainer to replace those hours in the car to the office every day.

"And, when I return, I will be ready to stake a claim to play for "Les Bleus", the French National team, and then on to our own Paris Olympiad in 2024".

Antoine smiled, took a sweet sip from his glass of red, rose and embraced his petite protégé. He could not resist her, and she, more to the point, could not resist hockey.

He thought, for all of us, there was nothing like playing.

Epilogue

Despite the onrush of geeks and computers in the sport, hockey revolves around personality, events and character. With that in mind, here is the chance for the readers to catch up, an update on the men and women that have filled these pages to prove they all have "Hockey in the Blood".

Gold: *Lav and Judy, after ten years as hoteliers in Folkestone migrated to his homeland on the Dalmatian coast to do the same. His only message was to the Author for wearing his K'rand dentures, a golden smile!*

Geordie Girl: *was cousin Sandra as the Byker Protégé, Gav was the Somerset "Geordie Girl".*

Malibu Shack: *Steven Faaronheigt's legacy lives on as the publishing wing of "That Ain't Hockey", and "Hockey in the Blood". RIP Partner.*

North and South: *Maddie is working the fields coaching, Michelle is the girl about town in London. Mojo inspires the next generation.*

A Canterbury Tale: *Roly is still very much part of the Canterbury street scene. Come on hockey folk, a helping hand?*

Oasis in the Desert: *'Maggie' works in a Windhoek bank in Foreign Exchange! She continues to play. Ted walks his beloved Downs.*

England's No 7: *Ashley is just married, and has stunned the hockey world by signing a two year contract with HGC hockey club in the Netherlands.*

The Reverend Blue: *Tony continues his mission as Bishop of Sherwood enjoying his role as the Ambassador for Sport in the Church of England.*

Three Aussie Sheilas: *Carol is married, a true native of Melbourne whilst brother Lance gets everywhere with 'Just Hockey'.*

Highway to Hell: *After a turbulent youth, all the boys moved on. Peter worked his career in Germany. Brother 'Fitz' was and is Gavin Featherstone.*

Dutch Courage: *Simon played in the Finals of the Euro Hockey League, and is thinking on one more year or settling back home.*

Homerton Home: *'The Fox', Martin Foxall at 71 years young still ventures out for his junior players in all weathers, at all times in North East London.*

When Hockey met Footey: *Bernhard remains the authority behind youth football academies in Germany based at Hamburg S.V.*

Last Tango in Paris: *Édith is on fire in her comeback, while Antoine lives in hope for her return!*

Index

You've enjoyed "Hockey in the Blood"?
Read "That Ain't Hockey"
Available on amazon.co.uk

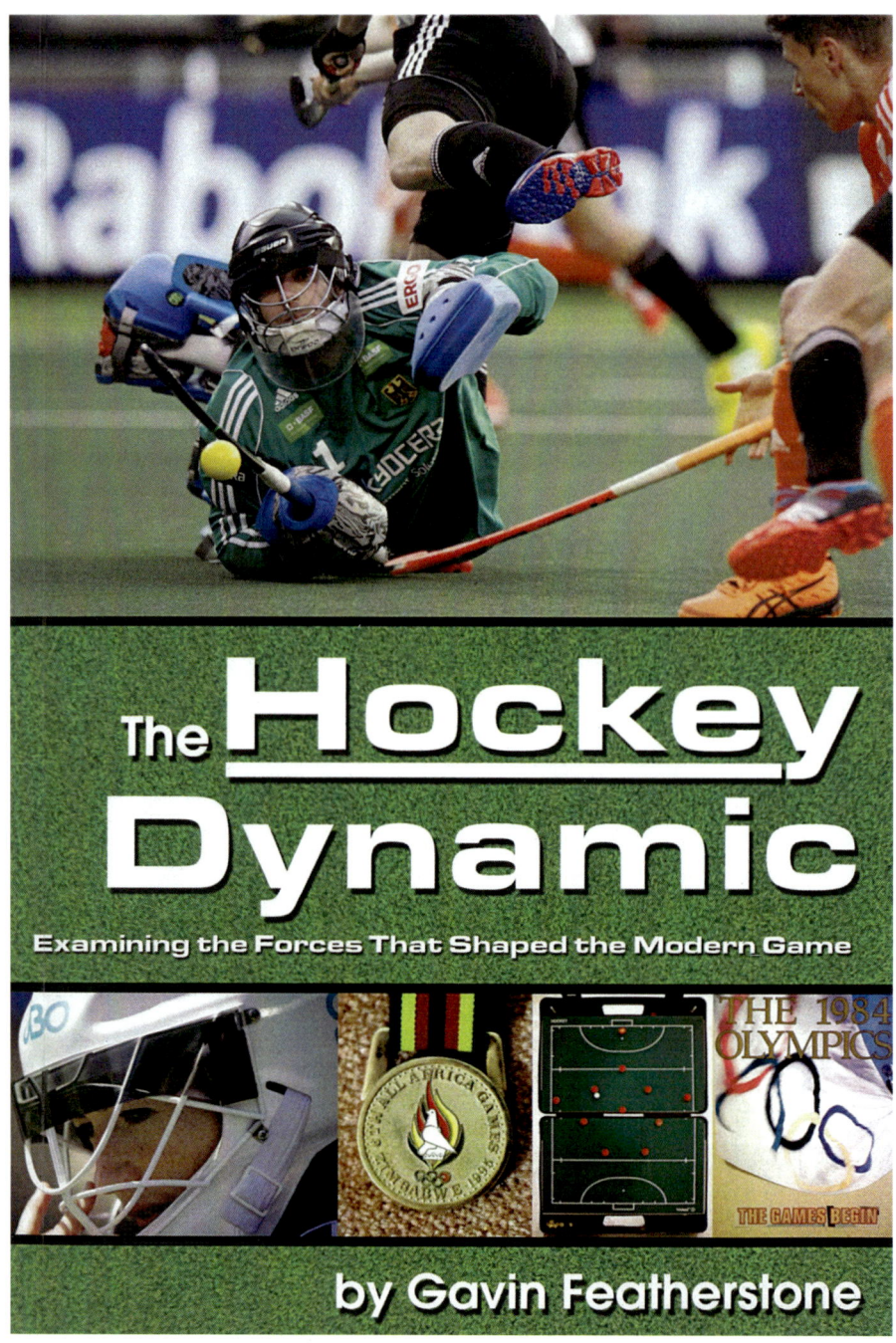

The Hockey Dynamic

Examining the Forces That Shaped the Modern Game

by Gavin Featherstone

You've enjoyed "Hockey in the Blood"?
We can always learn more!!
Read "The Hockey Dynamic"
Available on amazon.co.uk